Maddy Harland's regular columns have, in turn, offered inspiration, a shoulder to cry on, rousing calls to arms, space to mour̶̶̶̶ ̶̶̶̶ent and signposts to stories to sustain an activist's heart. They are ̶̶̶ ̶̶̶̶̶̶̶̶̶ ̶̶̶̶hered in one place, they offer a fascinating history ̶̶ its ups and downs, its breakthroughs and its epiphanies. in one place is a joy. Give yourself a treat, and swim in their deep, wild water.

**Rob Hopkins**
co-founder of Transition Network,
author of *The Power of Just Doing Stuff*, www.robhopkins.net

*Fertile Edges* charts a movement ahead of its time, whose agenda of growing the ethics of peoplecare, earth care and fair shares is ever more urgent and pertinent. These pages bear testament to Maddy's role beyond editor of *Permaculture* magazine as a teacher, author, activist, healer, visionary, nature connector, friend, community builder, feminine leader, systems thinker, mother, gardener and lover of life. Her voice of courage is a clarion call to anyone who has a rumbling in their belly, a hunger for a world of radical care and vital connection.

**Looby Macnamara**
permaculture teacher and designer
and author of *People and Permaculture* and *7 Ways to Think Differently*

Maddy Harland's work and life are an inspiration to anyone who dreams of devoting their energies to regeneration of land and community, and making a right livelihood from that work. As editor and publisher of *Permaculture* magazine, she has a global scope and more than two decades of her own thoughtful, protracted observation of the growth and development of the permaculture movement. A really valuable resource!

**Starhawk**
is an author, activist, permaculture designer and teachers, and one of the most respected voices for earth-based spirituality. She is the author of 12 non-fiction and fiction books, including the classic, *The Spiral Dance*.

About the same time Maddy Harland started penning this collection of essays, I went through a great change in my own life, leaving behind 20 years as a successful environmental attorney (punishing the bad guys) and embarking upon 30 years of permaculture teaching and design (aiding the good guys). Tracing her evolution through these pages I sense us as two vines curling up a trellis. As we reach the overarching part, Maddy has brought forth this truly amazing fruit. It packs lessons learnt along the way into nutrient-dense nourishment for the soul. Have a bite. It's delicious.

**Albert Bates**
author of the *Biochar Solution*,
*Pour Evian on Your Radishes* and *The Paris Agreement*

*Permaculture* magazine has served the good cause of caring for the land and for the people for 25 years under Maddy's editorship and leadership. Her editorials have been outstanding, I always read and enjoy them. Maddy's thoughts and words are timely, inspiring and filled with wisdom. I am delighted to know that these editorials are now being brought together in a book. It is a wonderful gift. May the permaculture movement go from strength to strength and may this book reach thousands of hands!

**Satish Kumar**
author, peace activist and
Emeritus Editor of *Resurgence & Ecologist* magazine

To look ahead, we are wise to pause and reflect on where we've come from. While reading *Fertile Edges*, we are repeatedly reminded of the unwavering resiliency demonstrated by Maddy Harland herself, *Permaculture* magazine as a business, and the permaculture movement as a whole. We have endured. We must endure. We do endure. Maddy presents us with countless tools on how to do just that in this immensely rich collection of timeless, insightful editorials.

**Cassie Langstraat** and **Hannah Apricot Eckberg**
co-founders of *Permaculture Magazine, North America*

Set against the enviro-political landscape of the past 25 years, Maddy's personal tale is fluidly woven throughout *Fertile Edges* showing a journey of growth and passion that has been reflected in the rise of consciousness of so many who have been affected by *Permaculture* magazine. The book reminds us of the importance of our individual right livelihood choices to influence our changing planet and provides hope and inspiration for our future.

**Ben Law**
woodsman, author and eco-builder

Reading Maddy's collected thoughts from over the years, as she raises her family, documents a growing body of knowledge of immediate and urgent importance, while observing humanity crashing and burning its way through selfish, absurdist, feudal, materialist collapse is breathtaking and strangely rollicking good fun.

**John D. Liu**
is a film maker, Ecosystem Ambassador for the Commonland Foundation,
Visiting Research Fellow at the Netherlands Institute of Ecology
of the Royal Netherlands Academy of Arts and Sciences
and Founder of the Ecosystem Restoration Camps movement

Maddy Harland's book take us on a journey through the past quarter century. Each insight, framed within the context of world events, politics and permaculture of the time, speaks to timeless wisdoms and reflections that continue to resonate in today's world. A treasure trove of gems of inspiration arising from the edges where the personal, local, national and global intersect and a glimpse into the life and mind of a remarkable woman and permaculture pioneer.

**Robyn Francis**
international permaculture educator, innovator, designer
and founder of Permaculture College Australia

It's an immense privilege to be asked to welcome you to this collection. Maddy's 25 years of endeavour demand our attention. She is knowledgeable, articulate and kind. In these pages she exemplifies the social justice that she says she inherited from Quakerism in a way that is totally non-partisan. Her strong sense of time and place and being ring out through her timeline placements of her work. She is a strong advocate for the role of women in achieving the changes we need. This book rings loudly with passionate truth. Join Maddy in her life's quest to impart vision for how we can create that better world and you'll be better for it.

**Graham Bell**
has taught permaculture on five continents,
lives in the oldest established forest garden in Britain
and has written two books and hundreds of articles on the subject

This book is a voyage of discovery, a witness for those who at times find themselves on the edge, and also at the centre of a quiet revolution. Maddy's skill as a wordsmith becomes a voice of our times, an inspiration and a beacon of hope. Whether you dip in and out of the timeline or read from cover to cover, you will experience a remembering and a message of hope to carry you forward.

**Christine Seaward**
leads an inspirational team of people
at The Sustainability Centre in the heart of the UK's Hampshire's South Downs

Maddy's passion for life in all its forms leaps off the pages and indeed one is left feeling that this passion has simply increased over the years rather than diminished under the weight of what appears to be an ever great crisis. No activist burn out for her. Along with the passion comes a deep embodied wisdom and an eloquence that enables it to be shared – or should I say caught as this is no simple intellectual exercise of knowing, Maddy has a knowledge that comes from every cell of her being. I encourage you to read this book and catch the passion and the wisdom.

**Professor Lisa Isherwood**
Director of the Institute for Theological Partnerships
University of Winchester

# Fertile Edges

*Regenerating Land, Culture and Hope*

## MADDY HARLAND

In Celebration of 25 Years
of *Permaculture* magazine

Permanent Publications

Published by
Permanent Publications
Hyden House Ltd
The Sustainability Centre
East Meon
Hampshire GU32 1HR
United Kingdom
Tel:      01730 823 311
Fax:     01730 823 322
           International code: +44 (0)
Email:  enquiries@permaculture.co.uk
Web:   www.permanentpublications.co.uk

Distributed in the USA by
Chelsea Green Publishing Company, PO Box 428, White River Junction, VT 05001
www.chelseagreen.com

Cover design Gail Forest Harland
Cover image, Ganges Delta © NASA

Text designed by Two Plus George Limited, www.TwoPlusGeorge.co.uk

Index compiled by Colin Hynson, hynson.nash@ntlworld.com

Printed in the UK by Bell & Bain, Thornliebank, Glasgow

All paper from FSC certified mixed sources.
The Forest Stewardship Council (FSC) is a non-profit
international organisation established to promote the
responsible management of the world's forests. Products
carrying the FSC label are independently certified to assure
consumers that they come from forests that are managed to
meet the social, economic and ecological needs of present
and future generations.

British Library Cataloguing-in-Publication Data
A catalogue record for this book is available from the British Library

ISBN 978 1 85623 309 5

*For Tim, for his belief in me.*

*For my daughters, for being my shining lights.*

*For Nature, for being my sanctuary and teacher.*

# About the Author

Maddy Harland was born and grew up in London in the Sixties, the youngest of four and the only girl. Her brothers taught her the Blues, rock 'n' roll and fishing; her father, drive and optimism; and her mother, a love of Nature. She was educated at Quaker boarding schools where she was taught the importance of social justice.

She is the editor and co-founder of *Permaculture* magazine, an international quarterly in print, digital and online at permaculture.co.uk. Maddy also co-founded Permanent Publications in 1990, an ecological publishing company, and The Sustainability Centre in Hampshire, UK, once a military base, and now a thriving immersive learning centre. She is a founding member of Gaia Education which developed the Ecovillage Design Education course endorsed by UNESCO. Maddy is a Fellow of the Royal Society of Arts and is a Visiting Knowledge Exchange Fellow of the Institute of Theological Partnerships at the University of Winchester in the UK.

© Don Wood

Maddy loves the sea, forest gardening, wild landscapes and adventure.

# Introduction

In 1992, Tim and I launched *Permaculture* magazine. We were living in a flint cottage in Hampshire and had a three year old daughter, Hayley. Tim worked on everything to do with production – editorial, typesetting and design – and I helped in the background. Our second daughter, Gail, was already on her way and was born in January 1993. We were also planting our forest garden and beginning to publish permaculture books. I remember editing Patrick Whitefield's *Permaculture In A Nutshell* whilst heavily pregnant. It was a fruitful time in so many ways.

By 1996, the girls were at school and pre-school and so I took over as editor. It seemed logical at the time as I had a degree in English and American Literature, a previous career as an environmental journalist and editor, and a Permaculture Design Course certificate. It was still very much a shared project (and still is to this day).

I started writing editorials on broader issues other than commentaries on the contents of each magazine. To my surprise and continued gratitude, my words resonated and I developed a following. More recently, readers requested I publish these editorials as a collection. With the magazine reaching its 25th year it seems like a good way to celebrate this landmark. You will notice that not every editorial is included. I have dropped a few that have not stood the test of time.

Why 'fertile edges', you may ask? In permaculture design, the edge is where the ecotones meet: the sky with the land, the woodland with pasture, the river with its banks and freshwater with saltwater in an estuary. These edges are where light intensifies for greater photosynthesis, nutrients are captured and biodiversity blooms. On the woodland edge, wildflowers attract butterflies, other insects and birds. The river bank is where silt is deposited. Trees seed there and cast their shadow and fish spawn amongst the cool watery roots. Tidal estuarine waters are full of waders feeding whilst pelagic fish, dolphins and otters hunt as the tide turns and saline meets fresh water. I love these wild places and I write about them in these pages.

I am also interested in the 'edges' of human society, where people fall between the gaps whether through poverty, illness or other factors that make them vulnerable. I believe that permanent cultures look after the vulnerable because they retain the threads that weave community. The web is tighter and people are less likely to fall through the gaps. Permaculture design encourages us to mimic the creation of edges to boost biodiversity and yields in land based projects, but it also helps us to understand social exclusion and design edges to minimise it.

The blood in my veins holds the DNA of the edge. My Welsh ancestors, the Dillwyns, abandoned their adventures in 18th century America and returned home to Swansea to campaign against slavery and to make their famous pottery. My Irish grandparents eloped to England, my grandmother being aristocratic and my grandfather unsuitably from more humble origins. My maternal grandmother and all her siblings were sent away from India to Europe by their parents. Being of mixed blood, they did not belong to any caste, British or Indian. My grandmother, a great beauty, ashamed of her Welsh/Indian descent, claimed to be Armenian.

Falling between the gaps is a theme in my immediate family. None of us quite fit any social milieu. This can make for lonely times, especially in childhood, as the pack can scent it. But it also offers a fertile perspective of what Albert Camus called 'the Outsider', the person who does not play the game society expects. History, even science, is deeply subjective and being an outsider has its benefits. It is easier not to swallow our cultural narrative or gullibly believe the 'double think' of vested interest that dominates our political and economic life. Instead, there is more space to think and breathe, to identify the ways in which society manipulates, to observe the twists and turns of mechanistic thinking, and the inequitable and suppressive nature of the status quo …

As we grow older we learn how to recognise those on the edge and appreciate that we are not alone. I have gradually met with my tribe and they are from many races and countries. They do not accept the narratives we are all taught but instead question conventional values and opinion. We share a growing kinship at the edge as world events become more critical and the danger of keeping things the same escalates beyond the conditions of survival for humanity, other species and entire ecosystems. These are quite simply extraordinary times.

Environmentalist and author, Paul Hawken, aptly called this place of extreme threat 'blessed unrest'. Unlike Camus, this is not an existentially meaningless edge; it is alive with the potential for activism. It is the place where new ideas and understandings emerge and intuition gives birth to practices that are eventually 'proven' to work. These ideas and practices are eventually adopted by the status quo who so vocally rejected them a few decades before. The people of the edge are habitually ahead of the herd.

Permaculture arose out of Bill Mollison's years in the Tasmanian rainforest, befriending and studying the indigenous people there, and his deep immersion observing the natural world as tracker, hunter and fisherman. It is an example of the fertility of 'edge thinking' becoming a global movement that brings together many different types of people. My writings here explore the emergence of that movement from the time I became the editor up to this, *Permaculture* magazine's 25th year. They are gathered together in sections that are briefly introduced and contextualised by world events and what was happening in the permaculture movement at the time. I also share some elements of my personal journey. In sharing them, my aim is not to take you to that grand edge, the top of the mountain, but to a place below the summit, where we can both look out over a landscape, and also upwards to the summit where we are still to climb.

" Permaculture is defined as consciously designed landscapes which mimic the patterns and relationships found in Nature, while yielding an abundance of food, fibre and energy for the provision of local needs … more precisely I see Permaculture as the use of systems thinking and design principles that provide the organising framework for implementing the above vision.

**David Holmgren**
*Permaculture: Pathways to Sustainability*

# Section One

# THE EARLY YEARS
# 1996 - 2002

World population is 5.766 billion.

**March 1996**, 'Mad Cow Disease' (BSE) breaks out causing a UK farming crisis.

**30 June 1997**, Hong Kong returns to Chinese rule.

**25 July 1997**, the Khmer Rouge start trial of long-time leader Pol Pot for the state-sponsored massacre of between 1 million and 2 million Cambodians.

**11 December 1997**, the Kyoto Protocol is adopted – the first agreement between nations to mandate country-by-country reductions in greenhouse-gas emissions.

**March 1998**, Serbs battle ethnic Albanians in Kosovo.

**April 1998**, the Good Friday Accord is reached and the Irish Parliament backs peace agreement.

**3 May 1998**, Europeans agree on single currency, the Euro.

**March 1999**, war erupts in Kosovo after Yugoslavia's president Slobodan Milošević clamps down on the province, massacring and deporting ethnic Albanians.

**February 1999**, President Clinton's impeachment trial for sexual misconduct is acquitted by the Senate.

**January 2001**, George W. Bush becomes President and in March the USA withdraw from the Kyoto Protocol.

**11 September 2001**, the World Trade Center is bombed.

**22 February 2002**, the Tamil Tigers and Sri Lankan government sign a cease-fire agreement, ending 19 years of civil war.

**23 February 2001**, Foot and Mouth breaks out causing a farming crisis in Britain.

**23 July 2002,** without the USA, 178 nations reach agreement on climate accord which rescues, though dilutes, the Kyoto Protocol.

**20 May 2002**, East Timor emerges as a new nation.

During this time in the permaculture world, we see perma-culture projects emerging in Asia, Africa and Eastern Europe backed by big NGOs like Oxfam.

Between 27 September and 7 October 1996, the 6th International Permaculture Conference and Convergence (IPC6) was held in Perth, Western Australia, attended by 300 people.

October 1998, *PM* moves to The Sustainability Centre, a former Navy Base that became redundant after the Cold War. It was at that time a shell with no heating and in the process of being converted to an educational centre in Hampshire on the South Downs.

In 1993, Permanent Publications publishes *Permaculture In a Nutshell* by Patrick Whitefield. It remains in print to this day and has been published in 11 languages, including Russian and Chinese.

In 1996, Permanent Publications publishes *How To Make a Forest Garden* by Patrick Whitefield and *Plants For A Future* by Ken Fern. Meanwhile, Bill Mollison, the co-founder of permaculture, publishes his autobiography, *Travels In Dreams*.

In 2000, David Holmgren publishes *Permaculture: Principles and Pathways Beyond Sustainability* that interfaced permaculture design with planned energy descent and was a key inspiration for Rob Hopkins and the Transition Movement. By 2002, Peter Bane, former editor of the *Permaculture Activist* in North America, estimated that 500 to 1,000 teachers had trained 100,000 people in permaculture worldwide.

During this period, I was adjusting to losing my father who died in 1995. Whilst editing the magazine and bringing up our children, I was also his executor, wrapping up a complex estate. My father was a Gooda Walker name at Lloyds of London. Their syndicates lost billions in the 1980s due to incompetent insurance underwriting and fraud. It was a salutary lesson for me in financial corruption. My father died owning uninsured, uncapped syndicates and owing significant sums of money. I learnt a lot about the City of London and its financial systems.

I was also learning about climate change and observing the ludicrous arguments of climate sceptics and a lack of political will at national and international levels to act. Even then, it was so obvious that we had little time to reduce emissions. Tim and I continued to develop our forest garden and I volunteered as a Trustee for The Sustainability Centre's charity, Earthworks Trust. We spent our holidays camping in Dorset and Cornwall with our daughters. Being outside all the time, rarely wearing shoes, swimming and surfing in the ocean, and making lifelong friends, these holidays were formative and blissful periods in the wilds for all of us. They provided much needed family time and a relief from the rigours of publishing.

# 11 | Spring 1996

As I write, Britain is in the throes of confusion over mad cow disease (BSE). Last week, Hampshire County Council issued a statement to all head teachers of primary schools that beef was safe for young children to eat. This week beef is off the menu. The country is faced with the mass slaughter of thousands of animals, an industry in chaos, maybe in ruins, and many angry and worried farmers and consumers.

It is a crazy system. Offal innocuously marked as 'protein' in animal feeds has been fed to other livestock. The disaster is BSE in cows and its consequence, CJD in humans. Incidentally, no organically reared beef has contracted BSE to date. But whatever we may think of non-organic and intensive farming, the way food is produced is a symptom of our culture, not solely the fault of one sector of society.

As a nation and in the European community, we expect to buy cheap food, usually dressed up in packaging, that does not take into account the health and environmental costs of the product or the well-being of the animal. Food miles, agrochemical pollution, factory farming, even 'factory shopping' (e.g. supermarkets) are the norm. Food is no longer a gift of Nature; it is a commercial product. It makes a lot of money, not always for the farmer, but for all the 'middle men' (and women) who take their cut before it reaches the consumer.

At the supermarkets, people now convert from beefburgers to TVP – veggieburgers are now in a bull market!

But is this a solution? Is highly packaged, marketed food, with ingredients often grown as cash crops in third world countries burdened with debt, the way forward? We don't need more products shipped in from other countries. Permaculture stresses the need to develop the local and bioregional connections: local farmers, local gardeners, local exchange schemes, vegetable box systems, community initiatives, resources (for construction, expertise, tools) and local marketplaces…

Permaculture emphasises the need to work with Mother Nature, not despite her. This is not an Arcadian vision or a denial of the value of many technologies, but a practical realisation that if we are to build a sustainable world, we cannot continue to foul our own nests, or our dinner plates. This Earth is an interconnected web of which we are all a part. We cannot cheat in one part to profit in another.

Einstein and Jung shared a similar theory: if enough people hold a vision, the collective unconscious, or critical mass of thought, of a culture can be influenced. We therefore need to believe in the pressing necessity of a cultural change and practically demonstrate that belief in our own lives.

Permaculture is unashamedly full of alternative ideas and practices. Most of them are for individuals and small groups, like forest gardening and other ways of growing your own food. Permaculture, however, is not confined to the garden, but in a society so disconnected from unadulterated food, it is a good place to start.

# 12 | Summer 1996

The permaculture theory was originated in Tasmania in the 1970s by Bill Mollison and David Holmgren as a system of ecological design to address the problems of environmental degradation. Its origins were rooted in soil preservation and creation and its focus was mainly on agricultural and horticultural systems, though never exclusively.

The growing of food has always been central to permaculture because if we have inefficient, polluting routes from the Earth to our stomachs, we cannot create an ecologically sustainable society. So the importance of people taking responsibility for growing their own food and producing other resources locally to reduce environmental impact is fundamental to permaculture. But as a system of holistic design, permaculture has always acknowledged the importance of whole energy systems. Houses, gardens and the wider community cannot be separated from agriculture and horticulture. They are integral to the energy flows of good design.

Permaculture design is based on understanding how the principles of Nature work and uses that knowledge as a model to design people and Earth friendly systems. But the knowledge inherent in Nature is very powerful and is not confined to growing plants. As permaculture design has evolved on the ground in all parts of the world, permaculturists have taken those profound principles and applied them to their own unique situations. It has become apparent that these principles can be applied to many aspects of life. Permaculture can also influence how we design physical structures: buildings, towns and village communities, and also relocalised economic systems (local currency and community supported agriculture projects, for example), businesses and social structures in communities.

Many people have discovered that working with human nature is often where the biggest difficulties lie. Fortunately, permaculture not only offers a holistic system for designing physical environments, it also carries many unwritten keys to reconnecting with a more natural, balanced human state through the deeply therapeutic acts of gardening, building with our local resources and working within our local communities. As we heal the Earth, we inevitably begin to heal ourselves.

In 1995 the High Court in England ruled against the planning appeal at the Tinker's Bubble project. The court defined permaculture as merely 'subsistence living', and by doing so ignored the real wealth of permaculture in an attempt to suppress it as a means of developing rural livelihoods. It is not enough to talk of 'sustainable development' and carry on consuming the Earth as we are. What is needed is a real cultural shift away from today's view of the world as a resource which is there to be exploited. Our reconnection with the land and Nature, both practically and spiritually, is the key to sustainability and ultimately the survival of our species.

# 17 | Spring 1998

Permaculture, with its attention not only to food but also to energy, housing and community organisation, has a powerful contribution to make to the sustainability debate. A few years ago, the word 'sustainable' was rather esoteric. Today, it is everywhere. What is worrying is the frequency with which this word is used, in contrast to the sparsity of action, nationally or globally, to solve the Earth's ecological crisis.

Let's consider some current statistics: we are using three times as much water globally as we were in 1950. The temperature of the air at ground level has been warming slowly and steadily since 1880. The 10 warmest years have all occurred since 1980. US oil reserves, by general estimation, will be exhausted by 2030 and world reserves of natural gas by about 2064. Scientists predict that if we continue to overfish our oceans many marine food webs will collapse within three to four decades.

The idea that we can go on as we are is a form of mass hypnotism. Yet when we watch television or read newspapers, we can be fooled into thinking that there isn't a global ecological crisis and that radical changes aren't necessary. The message is that we can go on consuming at current rates with a few technological changes – genetically engineered crops being one example.

Mystical tradition has long required that we 'wake up' from the limits of our egoic selves to gain enlightenment. Now a new form of enlightenment is required of us, and on a global scale. We have to stop divorcing ourselves from reality, but this is very hard – all the messages are saying the opposite – keep consuming, maintain material status and ignore 'doomsday' environmentalists.

There is also a tendency to take pot shots at permaculture. ("Most advocates apparently have no idea what is a fair return for a piece of land. They should give up armchair permaculture and practise straightforward allotment-style organic gardening … most practitioners of permaculture are doomed to near failure unless they can stomach a diet consisting mostly of shrubby spinaches." Bob Flowerdew, *Gardeners' World* magazine, January 1998). The impulse to shoehorn a set of ecological design principles into the narrow confines of a gardening method is irritating because it misses the point.

The essence of permaculture is that it is a holistic way of thinking which serves as a tool to create more sustainable ways of doing almost anything, from producing food to generating energy, recycling waste, designing companies, local currencies, community initiatives and whole communities – and linking them altogether. Permaculture is dynamic and in a state of constant evolution. This is why it is so exciting.

There are emerging permaculture movements in places that do not have the luxury of consumer choice, where food security is severely at risk and social disintegration is happening on a critical level. There are permaculture educational programmes and projects in Asia, Africa and Eastern Europe, backed by organisations such as Oxfam and Christian Aid. These NGOs see all the advantages behind establishing small-scale sustainable food and energy systems. I can envisage a day when we will awake from our state of mass hypnotism and realise that we have indeed run out of time and resources. Hopefully, people in other parts of the world will have learnt how to survive in a post-fossil fuel culture and the West will turn to them for their wisdom and innovative sustainable practices. Until then, we'll keep seeking solutions for sustainable living.

# 25 | Autumn 2000

The Sustainability Centre is situated on part of a former Navy base on the second highest hill in Hampshire. It comprises 55 acres of mainly mixed woodland, downland and areas fenced for pasture, and the South Downs Way runs along the edge of the site. The property is wholly owned as a freehold by a charity, the Earthworks Trust, and its planning consent is for an educational/training centre (which was its former Navy role – though the content of courses today is radically different!).

The Centre was set up as a flagship Agenda 21 project by East Hampshire District Council and was initially run by a seconded council officer. In 1997, this officer invited Permanent Publications to move to the site as a 'tenant ally' to help establish the Centre's presence and set up the education programme; this was with the full knowledge and support of the council's planning department and their legal services department. We toughed it out through three unheated winters (planning wrangles over the boiler chimney!), two changes of site management, and a council 'Scrutiny Committee' (to which we were not invited to speak, even though we'd been the only people who had seen everything that had happened on site every working day since the project's start). It was bleak at times, but *Permaculture* magazine itself continued to grow and also attracted people to join us as volunteers to help the site. Then in May this year, a couple came to live here and manage the woodlands, and two entrepreneurs arrived to run a woodland burial site and manage the pasture with sheep. Now, with council funding withdrawn and no centre manager, we have become a committed, self-supporting and independent volunteer force and this team is starting to make things happen on the ground.

In mid-July this year, however, Permanent Publications received a surprise visit from a planning officer and an enforcement officer (ironically, the latter was the same officer with whom we'd been in regular contact through the moving process from our house to the Centre in 1997). They asked us why we had not responded to a letter sent to us at the beginning of the month (which we had never received). They also stated that unless we applied for a 'change of use' (which they said was unlikely to be granted anyway) within 21 days of the date of the letter, an enforcement to move would be served. The words intimidation and harassment did cross our minds. It seems the argument is that in Navy days the site was 'apparently' a residential training centre and that planning had not been changed since then. Therefore being non-residents at a residential centre was in breach of planning. But there is a joke here … In the Navy's time, 3,000 personnel worked on site. Indeed, many naval staff and people attending courses were residents for their duration, but there were many others who commuted daily to the site along with the hoards of allied businesses who were subcontracted to provide services on a regular, if not permanent, basis. There have since been some attempts at negotiation, but as the situation currently stands, the 'change of use' is still deemed necessary and we are now being threatened with enforcement in November.

We find it hugely ironic that the publisher of a magazine all about sustainability (which has just been voted as 'the most useful resource for people wanting to live more sustainably' by a government funded survey, and whose staff have also given hundreds of hours of voluntary work to the project), is being threatened with eviction from a sustainability centre by a council that invited them there in the first place. If only all this wasted energy could be directed into something positive.

I hadn't appreciated how the Gulf Stream works and what a delicate mechanism it is until recently. Imagine that the oceans, from the Gulf of Mexico to the Arctic, are a vast, watery pump. Warm salty water flows north from the tropics on the surface of the Atlantic to the Arctic. The warm water heats our northern shores and, once it encounters cold fresh water from the melting ice caps, it sinks to the bottom of the ocean. It then flows back south, to return again and repeat the cycle. This cycle occurs because cold salty water is heavier than cold fresh water. If the water in the North Atlantic is too fresh (i.e. there's too much fresh water flowing from the Arctic), it stays on the surface of the Arctic Ocean and freezes rather than sinking to the bottom and flowing back to its source. What could alter the salination of the Gulf Stream? Simply, the increased melting of the Arctic ice caps. Too much fresh water dilutes the salty water and prevents it from sinking. The cyclical flow stops.

Last year, the USA and Russian submarines published ice-data which showed that between the '60s and the '90s, the two to three metre thick Arctic ice-sheet had lost 40% of its thickness, and 6% of its width. We're talking melting water here. In August this year, the Russian icebreaker *Yamal* ran through thin ice to the North Pole and its passengers were the first humans to see the sea at 90° North. Without the Gulf Stream, we could walk from London to Munich over icy steppes and rather than growing raspberries, Scotland would grow lichens over permafrost.

No more temperate northern Europe.

Scientific opinion on climate change is mixed but, thank God, it is agreed at last that it's real, not just paranoid environmentalists' imaginings. But scientists are divided on whether the potential climate catastrophe of the cessation of the Gulf Stream is real. It's happened before, however, 8,400 years ago when a great flood was released through Hudson Bay, caused by the collapse of the Canadian ice-sheet. The flow stopped. Temperatures dropped 6°C in Greenland and cold, dry, windy conditions spread across the northern hemisphere. What would it take to happen again? The US Goddard Institute for Space Studies predicts that it would take no more than an increase of 0.25% of fresh water flowing into the North Atlantic from the melting glaciers to bring the northward flow of the Gulf Stream to a halt. Even if it doesn't happen, we can be sure that climate change will continue, if we, as nations, go on haggling over agreed levels of carbon emissions and carbon tax and do nothing.

I'm not a scientist, so I can't predict the likelihood of a failing Gulf Stream, but I see this beautifully balanced natural phenomenon as a metaphor, an interface between Salt – Earth – and Water from the Sky. It's a magical cyclical alchemy enacted on our globe. To threaten its existence is pure madness. Our work here is not so much to save the planet – the Earth will surely survive our onslaughts in a changed form – but to save ourselves and the other swiftly declining species we are annihilating.

I remember as a kid going to Hampstead Heath on a Sunday and seeing an eccentric clothed in sandwich boards proclaiming the 'End of the World is Nigh' and dismissing him as a nutter. Much later, permaculture attracted me because it is logical, positive and personally empowering. But I have to admit that I am worried now. There's still so much denial about our impending global catastrophe and, even when accepting climate change as a reality, many still think it's up to politicians to make the moves, not individuals. Governments do not act, they react. We can't wait for that. Change has to be by urgent, vocal popular demand and it has to be NOW or else the man with the sandwich boards just may have been right.

# 27 | Spring 2001

Every morning as we enter The Sustainability Centre we have a salient reminder of agriculture in crisis – a vehicle barricade and the obligation to disinfect our feet to protect the livestock from Foot and Mouth. I can't help reflecting on the Industrial Revolution when we crammed people into cities without sanitation, clean air or healthy diets to feed the machines of Mammon. Vast profits were made, dynasties were established but at the costs of misery and human epidemics – diphtheria, typhus, cholera … The Victorians soon wised up to the causes of this and began a vast scheme of public works to clean up and sanitise the cities. You would have thought we would have learned our lesson about the consequences of industrialising living creatures, human or animal, and keeping them in insanitary conditions, but we obviously haven't.

Post-war government policy has actively encouraged farmers away from the traditional mixed farming system and into specialisation and intensification in order to raise productivity and profits. The result is that animals are reared in one part of country, fattened in another and exported from or slaughtered in another. After all, fossil fuels are cheap, so why not? Don't waste time growing feed and meeting the farm's needs within the farm. Just encourage larger herds, more stock and buy in all the feed you need – never mind what's in it. And while you're at it, ignore local markets, shut all the mobile and small-scale slaughter houses and ship the animals … where? Devon? France? Spain?

Cram animals in big trucks, mix up herds at every step, risking greater contact with diseases and to hell with the consequences. Make a fast buck. After all, this is the global economy, isn't it?

The trouble is that it's easy to blame government policy and the farming industry retrospectively, but at the root of the problem is our demand for cheap food. We want to eat mountains of processed grain, dairy produce and meat every day and pay a pittance for the privilege. But the reality behind real sustainability – not the buzzword or the spin – is that we can't. A return to mixed arable and livestock farming, even organic, will neither feed us cheaply nor halt global climate change. Unpalatable as the truth may be, conventional organic farming will not do the job alone.

The latest research tells us that ploughing the soil to grow grain (which is mostly for animal feed) releases $CO_2$ into the atmosphere, organic or not. Just consider that only 4% of our agricultural land in Britain is used for growing fruit and vegetables for human consumption. The great majority of the rest grows animal feed and rears animals for human consumption. The crux behind all this is the urgent need for us all to change our values and adopt more simple lifestyles. I'm not demanding that we all become vegan overnight, but to eat meat and dairy produce every day laced with exotic imported fruit and veg and processed food is simply ecocide.

Scandinavian researchers are seriously considering that agroforestry and permaculture systems may well provide the solutions to our agricultural problems. Imagine if, alongside horticulture, we developed agroforestry systems, alternative crops for food and fibre, permaculture farms growing food for local markets and productive home gardens in the city and countryside everywhere (all organic, of course). There is enough space to do it all if the current stranglehold on land use is relaxed.

I believe permaculture does have many of the answers we need to create a genuine sustainable agriculture, but if we, as a society, are still addicted to our consumer culture it doesn't matter how innovative the new generation of farmers become. The change must come from all of us.

Many people ask, 'Why is permaculture different from organics?' Permaculture can demonstrate, with real life examples, how permaculture is a process of protracted observation, based on the premise that 'the problem is the solution'. This is then followed by conscious design to create sustainable systems which imitate the qualities of Nature as closely as possible. These systems can be farms, gardens, villages, woodlands or communities, which harvest the energy within them. They are consequently as self-perpetuating as possible, whilst meeting the needs of the people and the environment that rely on their balance.

Organics is frequently concerned with food miles, with benign ways of generating power, with minimal imports of fertiliser into the system, but those are not fundamental, certified criteria. The main criteria of organics is the decision to use the natural carbon cycle, rather than chemicals, to fertilise and maintain pest control. This is no mean feat, but permaculture takes this a step further. It looks at the needs and wastes of the system as a whole and uses the design process to link them together into a cycle so that one element's waste fulfils the needs of another wherever possible.

In genuinely sustainable farming there is a great concern for growing feed and fertiliser on site, developing local markets and community involvement, minimising transportation, for developing many yields – polycultures – and for adding value at every opportunity. There is also a responsibility for recycling waste on-site (preferably into nitrogen-rich fertiliser), for minimising work by design, for harvesting natural energies like sun, wind, water and slope, and using space ('stacking') in a four dimensional way which includes time. The idea is to get as much out of a system as possible with minimal waste.

Permaculture includes farming, education, woodland management, woodland food, even natural contraception, and is all about applying these principles and ideas in real life. What underpins these examples is observation and thought.

I have recently been learning how 'energy follows thought'. This is not just a rarefied description of positive thinking, but an approach to understanding the flow of how we think, what we say and what we do. We create the situations we find ourselves in by our thoughts, attitudes, beliefs and sense of ethics. We then create the world in which we live, collectively.

I have observed how, much of the time, thoughts arise unconsciously and how speech and actions are often completed before we consciously connect them to reason. The problem is that negativities habitually arise, even when we don't really believe in them. The solution is to become more personally conscious and discriminating of our thoughts. Permaculture is a process of becoming more conscious, of understanding how energy moves in the physical world and of harnessing that energy in a creative and natural way. Its premise is that 'the problem is the solution' and its bedrock of ethics – earth care, people care and fair shares – are powerful thoughts with which we can undertake the improvement of our world in many ways.

We are a highly creative species and I have no doubt that we can invent, design, build and plant our solutions. I also believe that this process has to be supported by those three simple ethics and the collective thought that we can indeed make a better world.

In July, I watched with dismay, like many, the mounting violence at the G8 Summit. There used to be a time when anyone protesting against the WTO, GAT or power summits was written off en masse as 'rent-a-mob', purveyors of a sort of mindless anarchism, an indiscriminate kicking against any authority, and not worthy of attention. But this time we saw ordinary people – teachers, students, working people – being hurt because they were trapped between a seriously dangerous and out of control police force and a comparatively small minority of violent protesters. The mainstream media can no longer ignore that there are ordinary, socially motivated citizens who are deeply concerned about the effects of global capitalism and corporate might, or the fact that non-violent demonstrators were brutally beaten. The story is out, but at what cost? This escalating violence is very dangerous because it subverts by fear and intimidation our democratic right to speak and protest against policies and practices that we believe are wrong.

What has this got to do with permaculture? One of our editors once described permaculture as 'revolution by stealth'. We may not be overtly protesting on the streets but we are gathering together, with ever increasing coherence, a vision for positive social change, and a greater care not only for the Earth, but of its people too. Converting this vision into reality takes energy.

Our recent readers' survey (sincere thanks to everyone who participated) indicated that you are an energetic bunch of people. You want more practical ideas for reducing your personal environmental impact on this planet. We therefore start this issue with Patrick Whitefield's 'When Permaculture Strikes' – how to green your life wherever you are, before you have even stepped outside. We also attack the farming debate, giving you a living, breathing example of successful community supported agriculture in Scotland and evidence from Dr John Zarb that small-scale sustainable agriculture is not only possible, but highly productive. For the gardeners, we offer you the fruits of Clive Simm's wisdom on growing grapes outdoors and Christina Stapley's guide to growing and harvesting in the autumn garden. We entertain you with the concept of a post-modernist tinker (work that one out!), a strawbale building a Teletubby would die for and an update from Tony Wrench, deep in the Welsh hills, who is still suffering the slings and arrows of outrageous planning decisions. We also look at the increasingly popular trend of natural and DIY burials.

All these articles have a common thread – they are about taking charge of ourselves – how we live our lives, grow and buy our food, build our houses and bury our dead. They are about being active and making intelligent choices.

In an increasingly violent and divided society it is easy to feel those choices being eroded. The will to stand up and be different is constantly being challenged. It takes personal energy, strength and endurance to resist the spoon-fed consumer culture which deadens the mind. We therefore end with an article about permaculture and spirituality. In growing this vision of a better world, we need to also grow ourselves – to reach deeper understandings of who we are and why we are here. We need to be clearer in ourselves so that we can indeed make wiser choices, sometimes without much support or guidance.

I am, however, at pains to declare an open stage here. There must be room for all beliefs. There are many paths to follow and to be prescriptive of another person's beliefs is just another violence I can't condone. What matters is that our intentions are from the heart. Caring for the Earth just isn't enough. We need to care for people too, including ourselves.

It is sobering coming to work each day at *PM*'s office (once a military hospital) opposite a high security military base. It is even more so now as we pass military police on amber alert armed with submachine guns. They no longer wave. Their faces are deadly serious.

I recently heard that a chess master always aims to make the move their opponents least expect. I knew with sickening precognition that the terrorist attacks on innocent people at the World Trade Center would spark a predictable reaction – that fundamentalist mainstream America and Britain would use 21st century technology to bomb a war-torn country – and that the bombs could not be relied on to be 'selective'. They kill children as well as terrorists.

Humanity, it seems, is far from being master of itself. We protect ourselves in nation states polarised by their own cultural and historical perspectives, with proportionately enormous resources devoted to maintaining them at any cost, including war. By contrast, far fewer resources are dedicated to preventing or resolving conflict, or to generating deeper cross-cultural understanding.

Technology, particularly television and the internet, is waking us up to the fact that we do indeed live in a global culture. But with this comes responsibility – we can no longer behave like global village idiots. We need to acknowledge the absolute reality of our inter-reliance and connectedness, but we are doing the opposite. In the last 50 years, global crop production has more than doubled, yet half the

world's population is suffering from malnutrition. 500 million people are experiencing the danger of battle, imprisonment, torture and starvation. 20% of the world's population live in rich countries and consume 86% of the world's resources. Is it any wonder then that this global monopoly on materialism is making the rest of the world very angry? The killing of innocent people anywhere can never be condoned, but isn't it about time the link between materialism, greed and violence was made?

While the Dogs of War on both sides bay at us from our screens, Zach Goldsmith recently made a brief appearance on BBC Breakfast News to remind us about another act of terrorism, conveniently pushed aside by politicians everywhere. He pointed out that global climate change hasn't gone away. Rentokil report that the UK rat population is up 60% due to warmer winters. In 1998, the flooding of the Yangtze River displaced 56 million people. Hurricane Mitch killed 18,000. It will only take a further rise of half a metre before the Netherlands is uninhabitable. It appears that only a series of catastrophes in the West – after all, most of us only seem to care when something happens on our doorsteps – will alert us to the fact that the global crisis is with us. It has already begun.

In the midst of all this, it is easy to feel powerless and depressed. But what can we do? I believe we can do a lot and right now. I also believe that there are many thousands of people all over the world who are already actively working for

peace, reconciliation, equality, the relief of
suffering and a deeper understanding of
humanity. We each have particular talents
and strengths and permaculture people can
be wonderfully innovative and practical.
It is vital that we remind ourselves of what
we can do to make a better world and do it.
Let's not waste even one day being foolish.
Instead, let's harness those talents and be
the workers, the visionaries, the shamans
and the elders of the village. Let's escape the
alluring hypnotism of materialism, keep on
focusing on the constructive, regenerative
paradigm that must appear from out of the
rubble and let's support each other whilst
we are doing so.

# 31 | Spring 2002

Every year I experience the coming of spring with the deepest delight. I watch the green shoots of bulbs poking out of the snow, the blossom burst of blackthorn in the hedgerow, and the unfurling leaves of the great *Gunnera* emerge from its straw nest. The passionate and noisy revels of frogs in the pond in the front garden wake me in the early hours and the birds are enlivened with song and territorial business.

Life seems full of opportunity once again. Each year, my observations become keener and the experience intensifies. I feel a strengthening of a sense of place and the dissolving of the sense of separation – this is powerful medicine. It is nothing to do with observing the rare, the unusual. It is about deepening relationships with all living things, wherever we are, in the city, suburb or countryside.

One of the key teachings of permaculture is the relearning of observation. Our ancestors knew it well, but many of us have lost the art. It doesn't take long to get it back though – even the busiest people can find the time – and the rewards are great. Not only do we subtly develop that invaluable sense of place, the art of belonging, we are also rewarded with a greater reverence for the burgeoning life around us. Like children who can find the miraculous in the mundane, it makes us happy, and we need all the happiness we can get.

A serious and unhappy problem facing us in the 21st century is climate change. Research has proved that in the past century the average temperature has risen – in the south of England, for example – by 0.5°C.

Summer rainfall has decreased and sea levels are rising, threatening coastal habitats and the salination of water supplies, and increasing the risk of flooding. Predictions for the next 50 years are an increase in temperature of 2°C, a further sea level rise of 25cm, an increase in autumn/winter rainfall, more storms and extreme weather conditions, and a continued decrease in summer rainfall. We know that our flora and fauna will attempt to migrate north to adapt to the changes, affecting biodiversity, conservation management and farming; that some properties are already uninsurable; and that 'managed retreat' – a euphemism for abandoning lowland coastal defences – has already begun. What do we do in the face of massive economic, social and environmental upheaval?

I believe that we already have many of the seeds of solutions germinating in our creative minds. We have glimpses of the potential of agroforestry, renewable energy, new edible crops, integrated transport, teleworking, ecobuilding and community development. Sure, we don't have even half the answers, but we do have the ability to identify the tools we need to find the knowledge.

But what do we do about climate change? Is it the responsibility of world leaders, politicians, businesses or individuals? It is, of course, up to all of us, individually and collectively, but because the looming monster is so big our natural reaction is to turn away from the challenge. That's no surprise. But how about if we turn this on its permacultural head and say 'the problem is the solution' and that this is an opportunity for positive change?

We have a world full of things that need changing: wherever there is a blind obedience to self-gratification and the slavery of materialism for its own sake, we need to initiate change. And we already know that practices such as farming with fossil fuels are long-term silly, that partially controlled nuclear fission is crazy, that stuffing animals full of drugs, shipping them large distances in concentration camp conditions and then eating them is daft, and that killing each other is cultural suicide. But we can look at our own lives and say, "How can *I* reduce my ecological impact and live a more connected, Earth friendly life?" We can then take these values into our local community, our work, and question what our local politicians are doing to reduce a district's ecological footprint. We can demand that our national politicians stop bickering to score short-term points and address the issues.

What are the strategies for climate change? What research is being undertaken? How is this directly affecting policy in building, farming, manufacturing, tourism and so on? And from national accountability, we must then force the issue internationally. We have no choice. It all starts with our individual awakening which includes a journey back to reconnection and the engendering of a sense of place. Though climate change will be catastrophic for many, it will also be richly rewarding and the changes that must be made will contribute to making a better world.

Imagine that you, your family, your community are on a journey. You have travelled many miles and are becoming weary. You come to a fork in the road. The left hand fork is the easier terrain to cross. You have a map for this road. You only have a vague sense of the direction of the other road and you also assume that it will be difficult as it is an uncharted journey. The temptation is to take the left hand fork, but in the back of your mind you sense that it will eventually lead you down a path of suffering, to a place of devastation, beguiling though the short-term ease of passage may be. Some of your friends are arguing, they are tired and they don't want to think of the consequences of the unknown path. They want to go the way they know. Somehow, the decision rests with you, but you can't afford for the group to be split. You must seek consensus whilst persuading the others to take the harder, unknown path that is, in reality, the only logical option. It's your call. What do you do?

Whether you are a gardener, a healer, an artist, a soldier, a corporate magnate, a politician or a scientist, you are standing with the rest of humanity at this fork on the road to climate change and we do have a choice. What do we do? The left fork is the do nothing High Emissions (HE) road. The right fork is the do something Low Emissions (LE) road. Whatever we do, we have some degree of climate change, but let's examine the options using new UK Government data.*

By 2080, the annual temperature averaged across the UK may rise by 2°C (LE) and 3.5°C (HE). Winters will become wetter, rain and snow may increase by 30% with greater risk of flooding, and summers will become drier with risk of drought. Summer rain may decrease by 50% and average soil moisture content may decrease by 40% in the HE scenario. Sea levels are guaranteed to rise between 26cm (LE) and 86cm (HE) (10-34in) above the current level in South East England, for example, and extreme sea levels will be experienced more frequently.

What does this mean to our grandchildren or great grandchildren? Vineyards in Canada and Scotland? A Mediterranean climate in New Jersey and Lincolnshire? Sunny holidays? In part, yes. It also means a massive increase in desertification, crop failure, famine and refugees. It means huge economic and agricultural disruption. Cool temperate climate dwellers may be less disrupted (though inundated with climate change refugees), but no one in the global community will be unscathed.

I do believe, however, that the fork in the road that we are currently standing at is an unprecedented choice in humanity's history and one of profound opportunity. I also believe that this opportunity to make the right choice is the key to our evolution.

---

* *Data extracted from a UK Government Briefing Report,* Climate Change Scenarios for the United Kingdom *by Department for Environment, Food & Rural Affairs, the Hadley Centre (Met Office) & Tyndall Centre for Climate Change, University of East Anglia, April 2002.*

Do we choose the left hand fork – the high emission, selfish, short-term, ignorant path which necessarily shuts out the consciousness of the whole? Do we expect our political and business systems to only provide short-term economic gain and ignore the HE scenario? Or do we make a quantum shift in our thinking? Do we use our ingenuity as a species to serve not only ourselves but the survival of the whole? And how do we turn a doom-laden scenario into a vision of a better world? I believe that this critically required change could be the start of a more intelligent, humane, biodiverse and healthy world and that we have already devised many of the strategies to make that leap. Somehow we have to find collectively the key to inspire each other to act and, perhaps more importantly, to feel empowered to act (the principal aim of this magazine). And we have to do this, not in anger and desperation but with a balanced, dispassionate will. It isn't too late to slow climate change significantly. But will we take the right path? Of course, we must … but we will not be alone.

Permaculture – originally a contraction of Permanent Agriculture and Permanent Culture – is often viewed as a set of alternative gardening or farming techniques. It is true, permaculture is a radical approach to growing food, urban renewal, energy generation and water and pollution management. As Bill Mollison said, "It integrates ecology, landscape design, organic gardening, architecture and agroforestry in creating a rich and sustainable way of living. It uses appropriate technology giving high yields for low energy inputs, achieving a resource of great diversity and stability. The design principles are equally applicable to urban and rural dwellers."*

Permaculture's central theme is to create human communities that can sustain themselves and the landscape's flora and fauna within and around them. It is a whole design philosophy for sustainable living. At its core is the inspiration and example of natural ecosystems because the intelligence of Nature has so much to teach us. Permaculture has always been essentially innovative, trying and testing out new ideas, and pushing the edges of possibility. It has therefore become a philosophy of life for many. As such, it is rapidly evolving in coherence as people from different cultures all over the world take permaculture's ethics to heart and adapt its principles to their own lives.

In the nineties, I observed a growing movement to adapt permaculture principles (originally so often elegantly explained within a rural smallholding context) to the land-starved edges of the urban environment. Here the challenge is to evolve ecological ways of living in the city, where the majority of us on this planet are destined to live. This process of innovation is happily continuing.

In this new century, I see a growing need for permaculturists not only to discover sustainable ways of growing and building, of turning wastes into resources, but also to develop a philosophy of sustainable living which applies to our relationships with our fellow human beings. Whilst the earth care part of permaculture ethics has been practised with enthusiasm and vigour, the people care aspect has often waited patiently in the wings until we have worked out the day-to-day practical ways of living.

Whilst we haven't in any way mastered all the technology and techniques, both traditional and modern, for creating sustainable societies, our understanding is growing daily. What is becoming increasingly apparent and more urgent, however, is our need to understand ourselves and each other and to learn to live together in peace. Gardens of Eden cannot grow where tribal warfare and divisive ideologies prevail.

I believe that the time has come for us to explore the dimensions of people care within the context of sustainability. We are therefore starting this issue with a powerful piece of photojournalism, 'Just Listen'. This article is about an initiative in the

---

\* *Permaculture: A Designer's Manual* by Bill Mollison, Tagari Publications, 1988.

Middle East where people simply listen without judgement to the tragic stories of both Israelis and Palestinians and find that the act of compassionate listening in itself is healing. For me, this is the most moving article that we have ever had the privilege to publish. I hope you feel the same.

I remember some years ago walking across my native chalk downland in Hampshire with Australian permaculturist, David Holmgren. He has spent his life observing natural ecosystems, understanding the ebbs and flows of energy in the landscape, and applying those insights to designing sustainable gardens, houses, farms and communities. In those few hours, David taught me more about the ecology of my home through 'reading the landscape' than any book ever had.

He demonstrated why one of permaculture's fundamental principles is observation – observing Nature, observing seasonal changes, observing energy flows and so on …

Imagine now if we increasingly applied that skill of observation to each other, emptying ourselves of limiting preconception and just listening. Our observations would not be passive but active, our understandings would be transformative and our ability to place people care at the forefront of permaculture philosophy would be greatly enhanced. Most of us do not grow up with the privilege of being truly listened to. It is a skill that we have to learn and perhaps now it is time to gain that skill. In doing so, we consciously raise our game and work collectively, not only on innovative physical solutions to our ecological problems, but also on more subtle, but equally essential people orientated ones as well.

Part of the mythology that they've been
teaching you is that you have no power.
Power is not brute force and money;
power is in your spirit. Power is in your soul.
It is what your ancestors, your old people
gave you. Power is in the Earth; it is in your
relationship to the Earth.

**Winona LaDuke**
American environmentalist,
economist, and writer

# Section Two

# 2002 - 2006

World population is 6.234 billion.

**16 October 2002**, North Korea admits to developing nuclear arms in defiance of treaty.

**10 January 2003**, North Korea withdraws from treaty on the non-proliferation of nuclear weapons.

**5 February 2003**, US Secretary of State Powell presents Iraq war rationale to UN, citing its Weapons of Mass Destruction (WMD) as an imminent threat to world security.

**19 March 2003**, US and Britain launch war against Iraq.

**13 December 2003**, Saddam Hussein is captured by American troops.

**4 February 2003**, A.Q. Khan, founder of Pakistan's nuclear programme, admits he sold nuclear-weapons designs to other countries, including North Korea, Iran, and Libya.

**2 November 2004**, George W. Bush is re-elected president, defeating John Kerry.

**26 December 2004**, huge tsunami devastates coastal areas in Asia; at least 200,000 killed.

**9 January 2005**, the Sudanese government and Southern rebels sign a peace agreement to end a 20-year civil war that has claimed the lives of two million people.

**7 July 2005**, London hit by terrorist bombings, killing 52 and wounding about 700. It is Britain's worst attack since World War II.

**25 August 2005**, Hurricane Katrina wreaks catastrophic damage on the Gulf coast of the US; more than 1,000 die and millions are left homeless.

**10 October 2005**, Angela Merkel, leader of the Christian Democratic Union, becomes Germany's first female chancellor.

**5 November 2006**, Saddam Hussein is convicted of crimes against humanity by an Iraqi court, and is hanged in Baghdad on December 30.

In the permaculture world, David Holmgren publishes *The Essence of Permaculture* (now a website and download).

In 2003, Ben Law appears on Channel 4's 'Grand Designs' programme, building his Woodland House. It becomes the programme's most popular build ever and presenter Kevin McCloud's all time favourite. Permanent Publications simultaneously publish Ben's book, *The Woodland House*. It is our first contact with a more mainstream audience. Over time, the book sells in excess of 14,000 copies.

In 2003, Permaculture Research International director, Geoff Lawton, is consulting in northern Iraq, part of a team looking to rebuild a complete village destroyed by the Saddam Hussein regime 60 kilometres outside of Erbil.

Again in 2003, Rob Hopkins starts teaching 'Permaculture – Designing for Sustainability', a year-long course run at the Kinsale Further Education Centre in Co. Cork. It is the first time permaculture has been taught through the Adult Education system in Ireland.

*The Earth Care Manual* by Patrick Whitefield is published by Permanent Publications in 2004. It is the first temperate permaculture design manual that took Patrick eight years to write and bring to completion and Tim two years to edit, design and publish. It quickly becomes a game changer for the permaculture movement in the northern hemisphere, reinterpreting permaculture design for cool climates and is read and endorsed by people and organisations outside as well as inside the permaculture movement.

In June 2005, the International Permaculture Convergence (the first in nine years), draws over 100 designers, teachers, and graduates from 20 countries to the Istrian hill town of Motovun in Croatia. Harald Wedig presents his research into soil building with charcoal, an early mention of biochar.

In 2005, the Transition concept is born when Rob Hopkins and his permaculture students in Kinsale put together a detailed vision for a localised, low carbon town in 2021: the *Kinsale Energy Descent Action Plan*.

In 2005, David Jacke and Eric Toensmeier publish

*Edible Forest Gardens* Volumes 1 & 2, the first in-depth guide to temperate perennial-based gardening.

In 2006, Permatil in East Timor release *The Resource Book for Permaculture*, the first tropical permaculture design book. East Timor adopts permaculture as part of its school curriculum.

In the Harlands' life, our children are growing up, the first becoming a teenager and the second entering 'big' school. My mother suffers a stroke which leaves her with progressive vascular dementia but at this stage she is still determinedly independent. I go to Findhorn to a meeting of Global Ecovillage teachers and activists in 2005 and there we found Gaia Education, a programme that teaches the four dimensions of ecovillage design – ecological, social, economic and 'worldview' – a very permissive and open invitation to consider the spirit in design. The event and the people deeply inspire my work.

At that time, I am also studying healing, spiritual philosophy and to become a teacher of Esoteric Healing. I only ever hint at that side of my life in my editorials as any overt content in *PM* mentioning spirituality and the so-called 'non-rational' or non-scientific elicits angry letters from readers who say I have 'let them down'. Permaculture, still vulnerable to criticism for being untested and flaky, cannot publicly embrace ideas that involve the social and cultural aspects of life, let alone the spiritual, so my rich inner life is mostly circumspect. Yet these editorial continue to take shape and the values implicit in them are recognised by readers. I try and find a language that speaks to people of their worldview that is not prescriptive or dogmatic but opens the door to a wider perception of permaculture. This is one that firmly engages with the cultural aspect as well as the agricultural dimension.

I remember clearly when permaculture dramatically entered Tim's and my life in the form of a documentary series on commercial TV. Entitled 'Visionaries', one episode featured an outspoken Tasmanian, Bill Mollison, who was advocating a complete change in how we grow food, manage land, build houses and organise communities. He was a powerful and coherent prophet of climate change and the crumbling fossil fuel economy. He was acutely aware of the destructive nature of fossil fuel dependent agriculture and industry and had already started developing small-scale, practical solutions to mitigate climate change. Tim's mind went into overdrive and he hardly slept for a week. On a rare evening out together (our first daughter was newborn), he told me with great passion that he wanted to devote his life to permaculture – in his garden, his community and his publishing company. My post-natal reaction was one of fear and outrage! I had visions of toiling in chicken runs and editing muddy manuscripts … "I don't want to be a f***ing farmer's wife!" I said, as we stormed home, our first evening out in two years in ruins. I must have known that Bill Mollison was going to change my life.

I never did get mud on manuscripts, but my life did change. Tim and I planted a forest garden with native fruit and nut trees, soft fruit and perennial vegetables. We retrofitted a house, helped set up an ecocentre and a LETScheme, published new permaculture books and welcomed another daughter into the world. We also had the privilege of helping *PM* grow from a few hundred readers, originally mostly members of the Permaculture Association, Britain (the charity that helped us launch the magazine – thank you), into a publication with readers on all continents of this planet.

But rather than resting on our laurels, let me return to the passion and the storm. Why was I so angry about permaculture? It was because I was frightened. I knew intuitively that to embrace permaculture meant that I had to wake up to the state of the world and take personal responsibility. I had to expand my awareness, find my vision, walk my talk. I had to change. We all have to change. Therein lies the problem. There is a great resistance to it. However thankful we are for a decade of publishing, the growth of this magazine is still painfully slow. This reflects the difficulty when addressing the problems of the world. They seem so insurmountable. Even if we do cut carbon dioxide emissions by 60% right now, we will not start mitigating climate change – more droughts, floods, extremes of temperature, raised sea levels, more uninhabitable lands and refugees from the Equator – for at least 50 years. Scientists call this climate change inertia.

At a recent climate change summit, I watched chief executives and leaders of local government in the south of England resist grasping the nettle by initiating 'integrated' and 'far-reaching changes' of policy in agriculture and land use, planning and building specification, industry and finance. They seemed to be clinging to the hope that hydrogen fuel cells for cars, offshore windpower, home working and getting the public to consume less domestic electricity were enough. It wasn't that they were being bad or stupid, it was just that the problems appear to be so great. The solutions require new ways of thinking which may render our leaders unelectable – unless public awareness grows. The phenomenon that twins climate change inertia is cultural change inertia. The majority of us do not want change. It is too scary, too much effort and even if we do change, it won't affect us in this lifetime. By the time any mitigating effects are felt we'll mostly be dead and gone. So tackling climate change is never going to benefit us personally – it is an altruistic act – and altruism in our culture is definitely not sexy.

You, dear reader, by the very fact that you are reading this, do advocate change. So how do we influence a majority who haven't reached that point yet? I don't think we can do it by anger and confrontation, however frustrating the situation may be. Somehow we have to find common ground between people, learn the gentle art of co-operation and continue to walk ahead of the herd. This isn't easy and it can be exhausting. Make no mistake, I was right to have reservations about publishing a magazine on a subject that hardly anyone had heard of. It was a crazy thing to do (but thank you for helping us to do so). The fact that we have survived and grown indicates that the world is slowly changing. So our collective job is to hold the vision, support each other and keep innovating … Our job is to endure.

# 35 | Spring 2003

Being part of the team that publishes permaculture material is a privilege. In the course of our working life we hear from people all over the world. We share news of special events like the birth of a child, the joy of a new relationship, stories of far-flung travels and of new lives in different countries, even a different hemisphere of the globe. Inevitably, we also hear of personal bereavements and difficulties, and sometimes that personal loss is our loss too. This is very much about being in the midst of 'the stuff of life', as Shakespeare put it. It's often inspiring, sometimes gutsy, but always real.

I get an increasing sense of the common thread between all the people who contact us. There are strong aspirations to tread lightly on the Earth, to live creatively and develop self-knowledge – and to practise democracy and think inclusively, rather than to dominate, repress and alienate. Just as ecologists acknowledge the biological web of life, there is a growing sense of an ecology of spirit which is beyond national boundaries or political ideology. There is a growing realisation that we humans are interlinked. Despite a fear of Weapons of Mass Destruction, the popular consensus is that we must find more creative solutions for peace before we choose to wage war. As I write, NATO is divided and the UK and the US governments are increasingly isolated. I have no idea what the outcome will be before this editorial is finally published.

I have a deepening sense of unease about the West's global war against terrorism. Don't get me wrong, I abhor violence and fanaticism, but even the most superficial study of the history of the Middle East will reveal centuries of old empires and, more recently, new superpowers jostling for strategic dominance and mineral wealth. All this has divided ethnic groups and destabilised nations. Are yet more strong armed doses of Western medicine ever going to engender a world culture of peace and co-operation? I doubt it and I doubt that is its purpose.

I also have a growing concern following the Earth Summit last year. The Rio Summit in 1992 gave birth to much hope and so many positive initiatives. With Agenda 21, many people (admittedly mostly in Europe) actually felt that government was at last waking up to the positive transformational power of grassroots, community-based change. We hoped that the 2002 Summit would build on this, given that our scientific understanding of climate change has grown and that the need to change the way the world 'works' is becoming critical. This is a turning point in human history and our requirement to cool the planet is ever more urgent. Last year, however, Mr Bush famously sidelined the Summit and used it as an opportunity to pronounce on his global war on terrorism. A part of me can't help wondering if al-Qaeda (and Saddam Hussein) are, at least in part, being used as a huge political smokescreen, whilst we avoid the real planetary issues. Is it business as usual?

Let me return to a little microcosm, our network. I have been receiving letters and emails from all over the world telling me about climate change and specifically drought. In Queensland, Australia, citrus trees are beginning to die and home gardens are becoming less productive. In areas of India, water is rationed and it is still months before the rains come. Will they come in time? From rural Malawi, where outside aid barely penetrates, the letters are more heart breaking. They write of a two year famine, of exhausted soils and people so desperate they are foraging for inedible roots and berries and dying of poisoning. In a country that was sold the lie of the abundance of the 'green' revolution – i.e. monocropping maize with high input fertilisers – they are faced with exhausted soils and no means to buy fertiliser. They implore us to send money for food and drought hardy seeds to plant before the rains.

There is so much pain and suffering in the world that being open to it can become overwhelming. Yet there are also many people who, in their own ways, are working to alleviate it and live more within a consciousness of that interconnected web. So just as I am implored to act by others far away from me, I would make my plea to you now. Whether our countries go to war or not, please hold on to the thought that we humans are indeed intimately connected. We share a common destiny on this planet. Sooner, rather than later, we will have to devise collective ways of living more inclusive, democratic, ecological and peaceful lives. No smokescreen, however pervasive, can deflect us from that vision.

Permaculture's most defining quality is its practicality. Permaculturists are great composters of ideas, as well as organic matter. We take a broad range of technologies, skills and ideas and turn them into a rich humus of strategies for sustainable ways of living. Take the content of this latest magazine. It covers a wide range of subjects from Earth restoration, gardening, eco-building and renovation, to social democracy, climate change and Third World debt. It also includes ideas about the harvesting of one of our rarest resources in the 21st century – time – and examines permaculture in the context of human evolution. This issue is a window on the world, from the microcosm of the back garden to the macrocosm of global events.

We need to be brave to embrace both the microcosm and macrocosm and still remain grounded. It can be tempting to hide away in a Utopian vision or to be overly pessimistic about the state of the world and do nothing. We believe we have to engage in the world around us to grow as individuals and to play our part in the evolution of human society. We cannot retreat into our personal lives and ignore wider issues. Nor can we deny our own problems and escape personal responsibility for our actions by being solely outwardly focused. It is a question of balance. Permaculture provides a profound set of ethics and principles to live by to help us find this balance. Put into practice at a personal and community level, it offers a coherent framework for reducing our impact on the planet, individually and collectively.

At the core of permaculture is the understanding that natural systems are self-sustaining and that if we engage in active observation we learn from them. This process is not restricted to an elite set of permaculture 'designers'. It is entirely democratic and any one of us can participate in this process. Nature already has its own balance worked out and we are part of Nature. Through objective observation of Nature we return to ourselves and find our natural place. We can then begin to unlock the coherence and integrity of natural law that allows us insights into how we can harness resources, build fertility and create ecological balance. These skills are universal and they rest within all of us. We are all designers potentially.

Taken further, we can observe that Nature is inclusive. Left undisturbed, its cycles include not only fertility, growth and diversity, but also entropy and extinction – destruction as well as creation. Life isn't all light and birth, it is necessarily darkness and death as well, and there is a dynamic tension between these opposites. Both are necessary for the cycles to continue and for life to thrive.

In the environmental movement, there is sometimes a tension between the more vocal campaigners and activists – the holders of the 'wider vision' – and the doers, the gardeners, farmers, entrepreneurs and builders. Ed Mayo* calls these two groups

---

\*   Ed Mayo directed the New Economics Foundation between 1992-2003.

the 'stone throwers' and the 'alternative builders'. The stone throwers are engaged in breaking down structures that no longer work and are political, theoretical and overtly global in their thinking. The builders are busy making more sustainable 'forms' like ethical businesses, farms, gardens, houses and communities. They are hands-on, patiently working within their locality. As Ed points out, we need a synthesis of the two. We need the vocal, short-term campaigners and we need longer term testers of sustainable ways of living. They are different, but they are both valid forms of activism.

The reconciliation of opposites is part of the growing understanding of consciousness. I believe that just as human beings are evolving practical, hands-on examples of sustainable living, we also have to explore who we are, both individually and as part of the whole we call the human race in an organic and open-minded way. Thus I end by quoting David Holmgren from his recently published book, *Permaculture – Principles & Pathways*, arguably the most important permaculture book since Bill Mollison's *Permaculture – A Designers' Manual*, published 25 years ago:

*The deliberate design of a new spirituality that reflects ecological realities may be an unrealistic and dangerous extension of the permaculture agenda. However, an organic growth of spirituality from ecological foundations promises more hope for the world than the increasingly strident clashes between religious and scientific fundamentalism.*

One of the problems for all of us who live on the edge is that we can have a tendency to feel vulnerable and isolated. Criticism from within our 'group' can seem destructive, but as long as we hold our mutual quest for a sustainable world to the fore, we can welcome the stimulus of debate. We can differ in opinions and beliefs, but we don't have to pit ourselves against each other like party politicians. Please be reassured that *PM* will hold itself open to debate. Publishing is a group endeavour. We welcome and respect pluralism.

As a species, we have a long, long way to go in inventing systems of social governance which are fair and inclusive. One place where this work is being pioneered is in the ecovillage movement around the world. Not only are these communities ideal testing grounds for sustainable agriculture and gardening, renewable technology, ecobuilding and low impact living, they are also places where people are developing new ways of living and working together in harmony. This experience and its resulting wisdom is relevant to all of us, wherever we live. For this reason, we will continue to bring you stories from those who choose to live and work in groups in future issues. Meanwhile, I'll leave you with some relevant observations I particularly enjoyed …

## LESSONS FROM GEESE*

*Author unknown*

As each goose flaps its wings, it creates an uplift for the bird following. By flying in a V formation, the whole flock adds 71% more flying range than if each bird flew alone. ***Lesson*: People who share a common direction and sense of community can go further and get where they are going quicker and easier because they are travelling on the thrust of one another.** Whenever a goose falls out of formation, it suddenly feels the drag and resistance of trying to fly alone, and quickly gets back into formation to take advantage of the 'lifting power' of the bird immediately in front. ***Lesson*: If we have as much sense as a goose, we will stay in formation with those who are headed where we want to go.** When the lead goose gets tired, it rotates back into formation and another goose flies at the point position. ***Lesson*: It pays to take turns doing the hard tasks, and sharing leadership with people who, as with geese, are interdependent with each other.** The geese in formation honk from behind to encourage those up front to keep up their speed. ***Lesson*: We need to make sure our honking from behind is encouraging, not something less than helpful.** When a goose gets wounded or sick or shot down, two geese drop out of formation and follow it down to help and protect it. They stay with the goose until it is either able to fly again or dies. Then they launch out on their own with another formation or catch up with the flock. ***Lesson*: If we have as much sense as geese, we'll stand by each other like that.**

---

\*  Quoted from *Gardening With Soul* by Gaylah Balter, Learning Tree Books, 2003, ISBN 0 970861 1 5.

The nails are being firmly driven into the GM coffin. Last summer, public consultations in Britain revealed that only 2% of people questioned would be happy to eat GM foods. As Monsanto withdraws from Europe, another myth, that GM crops require less chemicals and therefore do less harm to the environment, bites the dust. Farm-scale trials conducted by the Royal Society have shown that GM oilseed rape and sugar beet actually reduce biodiversity. Remove bees from the countryside and you remove essential pollinators. Remove insects and seed bearing plants and we decimate bird populations and, according to English Nature, the skylark could be extinct within 20 years. Currently, the National Trust (3 million members and Britain's largest landowner) is balloting its members on a temporary GM ban and the Royal Society for the Protection of Birds (RSPB – over one 1 million members) is exploring the prospect of legal action if GM crops are approved.

So are GM crops safe for farm animals and humans to eat? UK animals are being fed GM maize fodder imported from the US. Reports suggest that most milk is contaminated – unless we buy organic or from Britain's supermarket chain, Marks & Spencer (M&S) – and the long-term effects are unknown. What is the impact of GM crops on soil ecology, from herbicide use or the genetic material itself? And what of cross-pollination? EU research indicates that it is impossible to grow GM crops without contaminating neighbouring fields. The trials did not address this despite high profile examples in the UK and Canada. Do nutritional values change over time? What about the incremental effect of GM crops grown in rotation over years? Lastly, and most crazily, the trials only compared GM crops with another highly damaging practice – conventional industrial agriculture. Organic farming wasn't considered. If there was ever a time to lobby government about ecological farming methods and developing a new agricultural policy, it is now.

Meanwhile, scientists researching the new edition of the *Times Atlas of the World* have had to redraw the coastline of Antarctica after the Larsen ice shelf, the size of Luxembourg, disintegrated last year. New evidence is emerging from the University of Colorado that the UN's Intergovernmental Panel on Climate Change have underestimated rising sea levels. "The IPCC thinks there will be an increase in sea levels by 2100 of between 1 and 23cm due to glacier melt alone. We think it will be nearer 23 and 46cm – and that's a conservative estimate," says Professor Meier. Glacier melt is only one aspect. Thermal expansion as a result of increased temperatures is an even bigger factor and both are part of a larger climate change picture of floods, droughts and extreme weather conditions that are affecting our planet.

We know there is a dramatic crisis on the horizon and that we cannot reverse it, even in our grandchildren's time. Yet when we read the newspapers or watch the television, we can be hypnotised into thinking that it isn't so serious. Furthermore, there is no intelligent explanation of the relationship between our fossil fuel intensive lifestyles – including profligate industrial agriculture (GM or not) – and the increasingly inhospitable nature of our planet. Put simply, burn carbon to eat, heat and fly about, poison soils, water and the stratosphere, and the lid of Pandora's box gapes open more widely by the day.

A friend recently asked me if I was optimistic about the future, given the state of the world. I am, because I believe that we are experiencing incremental shifts in consciousness that are small but significant. Psychologists compare human consciousness to icebergs. We have at most 10% of our group consciousness rising above the surface of the water. The rest is hidden. They also believe that it only takes 17% of a group to influence the opinion of the remaining 83%. In other words, the critical mass of a group is far lower than the majority. I believe that critical mass is being reached with GM in the UK and this will force a more democratic and considered agricultural policy from government. Critical mass is still lagging behind on climate change. But when we reach 17% of people who understand the total necessity of living sustainably and reject our current destructive paradigms, then the shift will come very fast. Now is the time to become increasingly vocal, and not only about expressing the serious nature of our problems. We also have the privilege of presenting a rich collage of solutions, many in their infancy. We have to be patient, we have to

be measured, and we have to be persistent, but have no doubt, now is the time to protest to survive. So please, write to your government representative and preferred newspaper, and pull the debate into the mainstream.

I have, like many others, been observing the Weapons of Mass Destruction (WMD) controversy with an increasing sense of inevitability. So many people in the West suspected that WMD were a flimsy excuse for war with Iraq and yet, despite huge peace protests all over the world, there was nothing anyone could do to stop the war machine. But whatever your politics are about the war itself, let's look at WMD from the ecological perspective of Depleted Uranium (DU). DU is a highly toxic heavy metal derived from nuclear bomb and fuel waste (also containing plutonium and other fission materials). The United Nations classifies DU weapons as 'weapons of mass and indiscriminate destruction'. Their use, according to an August 2002 report by the UN subcommission, breaches the Universal Declaration of Human Rights, the UN Charter, the Genocide Convention, the Convention Against Torture, the Four Geneva Conventions of 1949 ... and so on. DU is an effective and cheap nuclear weapon, used in tank and artillery fire shells as a powerful way of penetrating and destroying metal. The shells are like a firestorm of lightning on nearby victims and structures, insignificant compared to a nuclear bomb, but on impact DU pulverises people, tanks and buildings and the dust, fragments and smoke can travel miles. It remains radioactive for millions of years and contaminates the air, soil and water.

Because the dust is so fine, it acts like a gas, seeping through protective masks. If inhaled it can cause cancer, chronic illness, long-term disabilities and birth defects. DU has been blamed for Gulf War Syndrome, and in southern Iraq where DU was fired in 1991, childhood leukaemia rates have increased six to ten fold and birth defects between four and six fold in the intervening years, according to the UN subcommission. Studies of children subsequently born to Gulf War veterans showed an alarmingly high incidence of birth defects. The Pentagon claims that 320 metric tonnes of DU were left on the battlefield after the first Gulf War (the Russians say it was nearer 1,000 tonnes). In last year's conflict between 1,100 and 2,200 tonnes were fired. A UK Atomic Energy Authority report estimates that 500,000 people will die due to radioactive debris left in the desert.

So there we have it – evidence of WMD at last – or should we call them Weapons of Mass Hypocrisy? Because, yes, it was the British and Americans who used them. They also used them in conflicts in Bosnia, Kosovo, Macedonia and Serbia. All this despite the fact that there is evidence as far back as 1984 that the US Navy knew of the dangers of DU contamination.[*] These munitions were apparently tested in the Solway Firth, Scotland (6,350 rounds fired, 1989-99) and in seven US states. Professor Doug Rokke, ex-director of the Pentagon's DU project and a former

---

[*]  http://slwater.iwmi.org/sites/default/files/DocumentRoot/Ur.pdf

professor of environmental science, describes the use of DU as a 'crime against humanity'. He calls for the UK and US "to recognise the immoral consequences of their actions and assume responsibility for medical care and thorough environmental remediation. We cannot just use munitions which leave a toxic wasteland behind them and kill indiscriminately."* Public awareness of this human and environmental travesty is growing and the International Coalition to Ban Uranium Weapons is launching a full-scale international campaign in May this year.**

I have a strong belief that we have differing paths to follow. As people seeking more sustainable and peaceful ways of living, we may not wish to, or even be able to, extend our work beyond our local communities – the work we do is hard enough. But whilst we are toiling in our own particular niche, I believe it important that we extend our support, be it at times only morally, to others who are working directly to uncover the hypocrisy and immoralities at large in our complex and unsustainable world. We owe it to ourselves and humanity as a whole to endeavour to lead responsible and ecologically balanced lives. We also have to expand our awareness – of the good and the bad – without destabilising our resolve and positive visions for the future.

*   www.sundayherald.com
**  www.bandepleteduranium.org

Three years ago I wrote an editorial about the exquisite, intelligent mechanism of the Gulf Stream which operates like a vast global pump, driven by a delicate balance between salt and fresh water (see page 11). Warm salty water flows north from the tropics on the surface of the Atlantic to the Arctic. It heats the northern shores of North America and then meets the cold fresh water of the melting ice caps, and sinks to the bottom of the ocean because the warm salty water is heavier than the cool melt water of the Arctic. It then flows back south where the cycle starts again. The flow is determined by the balance between heat, cold and salinity. Too much melt water, and the surface of the ocean becomes too cold and dilute and freezes over. The pump stops and an ice age dawns. The Gulf Stream failure is the subject of a Hollywood film, *The Day After Tomorrow*, directed by Roland Emmerich (*Independence Day* and *Godzilla*). We have a green epic with all the sensation of the instant apocalypse. Los Angeles is ripped apart by tidal waves, New Yorkers swelter in a fatal heatwave and are then plunged into glacial freeze as the Gulf Stream fails in a single day, and New Delhi is confounded by severe snowstorms whilst Tokyo is bombarded by hail stones the size of grapefruit. Already, the film is having its impact. Commentators are predicting that it will alert Americans in election year to the fact that President Bush has ignored the greatest crisis humanity has ever faced. Should we welcome this film? I am relieved that the world is waking up but I worry that sensationalising climate change will do

two things. Firstly, it may make people take the slower, less instantly catastrophic reality less seriously. Yes, we know the weather is becoming more extreme, causing floods, droughts, heat waves, crop failures, epidemics of mosquitoes causing malaria and dengue fever – but we'll find a way to slot it into a manageable, 'it isn't so bad' scenario. Also by sensationalising climate change, many people may be tempted to relegate the reality into a fiction.

But business and governments are gearing up for change. Already, the futures market is mapping the changes to the wine industry. Grapes are apparently a good indicator crop. As Europe gets hotter, we obsessively taste and rate them for quality. The predicted temperature rise is likely to make cooler regions better producers of some grape varieties and already warm wine regions less hospitable, changing the vintners' viticultural map forever. The sheltered chalky slopes of my home could become hot viticultural property. Then there's the financial impact. Swiss Re, the world's second largest reinsurer, is talking about climate change costing US$150 billion (£81 billion) a year in 10 years, hitting insurers with US$30 - 40 billion in claims – the equivalent to insurance payouts on one World Trade Center attack per annum. Last year was Europe's hottest in at least five centuries and nearly 19,000 people died. France was hardest hit and the French Government has now asked its workers to sacrifice one day's holiday a year to help finance state care for the elderly and the disabled who are naturally more vulnerable in heatwaves. Then, according to the Earth Policy Institute, world grain stocks are reported to have fallen to their lowest level in 30 years as climate change wreaks havoc with production, threatening severe hunger in countries short of food.

My second concern is that as we become increasingly aware of the reality of climate change, we will feel a greater sense of disempowerment. Can we really do anything to adapt, let alone mitigate this change? Without global political will, what can we do as individuals? What are the realistic and practical solutions? Talking recently with author and teacher, Patrick Whitefield, we agreed that anything we do as individuals can only be part of a greater whole. The actual outcome of what each of us does depends on the actions of lots of other different people. We can't take responsibility for the results but we can maintain, like Gandhi, a non-attachment to the fruits of our labours. As Patrick puts it, "The important question is not, 'Am I going to succeed?' The important question is, 'How am I going to live my life?' The only thing I can say is that I have played my part in a way that is right. I would rather be a part of the solution than part of the problem." I am not a Buddhist but I have long admired the concept of 'Right Livelihood'; that if we chose to live and work in peaceful and harmless ways, this is the noble way to live. My instincts tell me that as the debate escalates and events on our planet become more extreme, we will need to work from this calm centre of non-attachment and that this approach will give us a wiser and a more stable perspective.

I have been lucky to have been invited to meetings in two ecovillages, Findhorn in Scotland and ZEGG in Germany this year, both well established communities. In both places I found differing yet wonderful examples of sustainable living: community supported agriculture; a natural swimming pool (gorgeous to swim in on a hot day!); beautiful edible landscapes; examples of new and renovated ecobuildings; sculptures, mosaics and paintings integrated into the community spaces; music; biological sewage treatment areas full of plants, trees and cleaned water; areas of sanctuary for rest and reflection and an array of renewable energy – photovoltaics, solar water, wood chip boiler, a community owned wind turbine. ZEGG even has its own pub, open each evening, as well as a bigger space for screening films and clubbing. Every Saturday night, villagers and neighbours gather together to have a good time. Visitors can also join in the fun!

It is inspiring to see all these ecological techniques and experiments gathered together in just two communities, meet the villagers and sample the fine organic and ethically sourced cuisine. The range of successful micro-businesses also impressed me – shops full of community and locally made jewellery, good books, organic food, crafts, photography and art – potteries, ecological consultancies, tailors, nurseries … I also had the pleasure of witnessing the skilled facilitation of meetings, the level of care for people in the communities (both visitors and residents) and innovative methods of conflict resolution and

decision-making. I do not want to convey to you that these are utopias. They are places of experimentation, for buildings, technology and growing both food and people. Inevitably there are lessons to be learnt, internal and external conflicts with the neighbours to be resolved. These are places, however, of transition where I found not only ecological hope for the future but also, and perhaps more importantly, tools for the creation of peaceful relations between people. Surely, the most unsustainable aspect of our world is the conflict between us, as individuals and as groups, from small communities to nations? It gives me heart to experience at first hand positive intention and co-operation between people and genuine efforts to understand and transform the wars within ourselves. This inner work is vital. An ecologically balanced community cannot be the whole story – its people also need to be working towards harmony and balance.

There has been much to learn in the last few months. Whilst at Findhorn, I was introduced to a simple set of community guidelines that can be used in any circumstance where people meet and work together. I take this opportunity to share them with you and hope you find them as useful as I have. First, practise the art of personal presence. Embrace the tensions of opposites and tolerate and encourage the abstract, the unexpected and the discomfort of expanded consciousness. Second, practise Mudhita, the ageless Buddhist practice that is the other side of the coin of compassion; identify with the joy, gifts, pleasures and awakenings of others. This is the art of vicarious joy that banishes cynicism and envy. Third, make your communication mindful and compassionately brief. Be appropriate, both on a one to one basis and with the whole group. Four, do not 'triangulate' – if we have issues or conflicts we should clear them with the individual concerned and not report to others. This is all about cultivating a culture of direct communication rather than gossip. Five, practise punctuality. Time is limited. It demonstrates a respect for group process. Six, practise consensus by default, perhaps the most difficult ideal to achieve at all times.

So are we relocating to an ecovillage? It is tempting, I can tell you. Life in the mainstream can be lonely and frustrating. It has taken years to feel a sense of acceptance and belonging in my own village but my children are happily integrated and we now have many friends. Then there is the team, both at *PM* and at The Sustainability Centre here, to whom we all hold our allegiance and the potential of being part of the creation of a good project too. Many of us have to do it where we are, even though the prevailing culture may seem light years away from greening their vision. But I suspect that the effects of climate change and human conflicts will demand change and we will collectively have to face the fact that the transformation will be, out of necessity, social as well as ecological.

I recently gave a slide show on permaculture to a local horticultural group and amid photographs of ecobuilding, forest gardens, fruiting figs and heritage apples I popped in a picture of a nuclear power station and raised the question of energy decline.

At the end of the presentation a beady-eyed elderly woman approached me and asked, "How many nuclear power stations do we need to supply the whole of Britain?"

"Six," I answered.

Her eyes gleamed.

"And how many wind generators do we need?"

"Wind power can supply approximately 24% of our total electricity consumption in Britain," I replied.

"Ha, so renewable energy can't do the job," she crowed. "We have to have nuclear and nuclear power is cheap and clean."

"But with renewables we are not looking to substitute large-scale generation," I answered. "Besides wind, there is the potential of hydro-electric, biomass, photo-voltaic and tidal, and these can be individual installations, town-scale or larger. The most important approach is the conservation of energy – we waste huge amounts. Then nuclear has never been found to be economically viable. Finally, it certainly isn't 'clean'. What about the waste?"

"Well," she retorted, "we can dump it in the sea. It breaks down in 500 years."

"The half life of plutonium certainly isn't 500 years, it is 24,000 years and you can't just dump it in the sea! The Irish Sea is one of the most radioactive seas in the world due to Sellafield's dumping programme. And what about the high incidence of cancer clusters around Sellafield?" I was getting rather hot under the collar by this time.

"Well, we don't have to live there!" she replied.

"Is it acceptable to have levels of childhood leukaemia far above the national average there as long as it isn't affecting your grandchildren?"

She was momentarily quiet and then retorted, "Well, what about nappies then? They don't break down in the ground for 500 years either."

Two things struck me from this encounter. Firstly, that people are beginning to accept climate change and the end of fossil fuel energy as a reality. Even the notorious British tabloid newspapers are now reporting on it. Then there is the natural assumption that we have to substitute one for one – wind generated electricity for fossil fuels – and this isn't feasible so the logical conclusion is to advocate nuclear. But this is linear thinking (listen up James Lovelock and David Bellamy). We cannot solve our impending energy crisis by replicating the same paradigms with different energy sources. Change is inevitably in the air and we should welcome it. Our ability to innovate in the renewable energy field is still at a very early stage. There is much left to discover – witness the work at Tamera Peace Research Village in 'Grassroots Solar Solutions' in this issue – but once we climb out of the large-scale industrial box, we can begin to think more creatively.

Our approach to energy systems has

to be multi-dimensional, from individual panels like the one featured in 'Sun & The City' (see this issue), to community-scale systems (including hydro-electric), to town-scale biomass programmes and only then, when we have maximised our local potential, should we consider larger installations. But the first line of attack has to be conservation of energy **everywhere** – at home, school, work, at leisure, corporately … We also have to acknowledge the reality of our energy decline. We have lived off the fat of fossil fuel and it is (thankfully) running out, though not before we have altered the climate irreparably. Society will have no choice but to fundamentally change. Will it be with force and aggression or with co-operation and a growth in consciousness? Ever the idealist, I would love to see a more evolved, compassionate, intelligent and just society and am weary of the rabid consumerism and selfishness that seem to be the current keynotes of our world.

The week before my encounter with the 'nuclear' lady I'd led a workshop on media activism, the gist of my introduction being that we are more effective when we work from a point of heart/brain coherence. Instead of reacting instinctively when under pressure, we can train ourselves to regulate our heartbeat by 'breathing through the heart' and use visualisation to collect ourselves in times of stress. This is a place of detachment. We know the issues, we feel the passion, we do the work, but we can be more effective working from a place of peace rather than from anger and frustration. We want to encourage a growth of awareness, not argument and confrontation. Better that our heart rate is regular, our brains responding creatively rather than instinctively, and we retain a sense of proportion and calm. That's the theory, but it takes practice – every day – and that elderly woman certainly put me to the test!

# 43 | Spring 2005

Tim and I started a book publishing company in 1990 and launched *PM* in 1992. The team has changed over the years, except for two constants, Tim and myself, but the message has not altered. The vision is still to publish material that empowers and encourages people from all walks of life to make a difference; to take serious account of the many worsening ecological and social problems in our world and seek out solutions; and to believe in the fundamental possibility of goodwill and its power to transform people and their environments.

In the last three months, there seems to have been a quantum shift in the world and this vision is severely challenged. Not a day goes by without yet more media commentaries, films, scientific reports and conferences about escalating climate change. It is easy to become bewildered by the bad news; the apparently conflicting sciences of global warming and global dimming (caused by jet aircraft's vapour streams which reduce the planet's surface temperatures); the reports that climate change is now out of control – we have gone beyond the point of reversal; and the awful dawning reality that, now the USA controls the oil reserves in Iraq and the piping route through Afghanistan from the Caspian Sea, Iran is the next target in the Carbon Wars. All this is the direct consequence of our pathological addiction to dwindling carbon resources. However many oil fields the US/UK alliance annex, the predictions are that within less than a generation, there will be extreme price rises and dire shortages.

This will affect every aspect of our Western infrastructure and lifestyle well before we run out. Our murderous scramble for oil is taking place in full political knowledge of Peak Oil and with our electoral consent.

Now this may sound gloomy, but what I am moving towards are a number of psychological strategies that will enable us to face facts and still stay positive and focused. It is all too easy to engage in displacement activities, seal off a part of ourselves and become isolated, imbibe mind numbing substances or get angry and project all that sense of disempowerment and despair onto others. We cannot infuse a world with goodwill and ethical values from a state of rage. It is also easy to feel depressed and powerless. "What is the point of … when I can make no difference?" Personally, I try to live my life one day at a time with new eyes, whether I am stacking next winter's wood, mulching veggie beds, teaching or publishing. Gary Zukav describes this practice in *The Dancing Wu Li Masters*: "Every lesson is the first lesson. Every time we dance, we do it for the first time … When I say that every lesson is the first lesson, it does not mean that we forget what we already know. It means that what we are doing is always new … This is another characteristic of a Master. Whatever he does, he does with the enthusiasm of doing it for the first time. This is the source of his unlimited energy. Every lesson that he teaches (or learns) is a first lesson. It is always new, personal and alive." I am no 'Master', but this practice sustains me. There is joy in it.

I also know that whatever my intuitions may be, neither I nor anyone else can accurately predict the future. Therefore, I choose to act 'as if' – *as if* we will soon look at the George W. Bush/Tony Blair administrations, marvel at the madness of the Carbon Wars and finally say 'no'; *as if* there will be a global awakening to our ecological predicament and radical changes implemented with unprecedented insight and wisdom; *as if* my small life makes a difference, not as one individual, but because I am part of a group which is acting *as if* and encouraging others to do so; *as if* it is not too late … The days of passivity are over and we are no longer here to be led. We are the leaders. This new form of leadership is not about dominance, control or cynically harvesting the resources of others. It is about learning how to work together in groups, unlocking our collective potential, diversity of skills and experiences, and synthesising these resources into effective action. The power is in the numbers. I am acting *as if* every day our numbers are growing – and they are. In this permaculture microcosm, we now have more subscribers worldwide than ever before. I am not denying the complexity of the problems or how difficult and painful it is to overcome conflict and stay engaged. We must 'hear within us the sounds of the Earth crying', as Thich Nhat Hanh said, and still have the courage and tenacity to carry on. *As if…*

My last editorial was about living in the 'now', trying to greet every experience with fresh eyes, and acting in good faith in the hope that our collective actions can make a difference. You know what it is like when you open your mouth or commit yourself on paper?! You get tested – and I did. What made me stumble were the recent updates from the UN's Intergovernmental Panel on Climate Change (IPCC) at an international conference called by Tony Blair. The international community of sombre climate scientists reported in their third assessment report that the Earth's average surface temperature is likely to warm by 1.4-5.8°C between now and 2100, depending on how successful we are in curbing carbon emissions. Given that the US (the biggest atmospheric polluter) has rejected the Kyoto Agreement, that China and India are experiencing huge economic growth (and subsequent rises in $CO_2$ emissions) and that our European commitment to cut $CO_2$ is paltry (under 5% of 1990 levels), there isn't much hope.

We are on course for a global crisis of unprecedented destruction. The British Antarctic Survey reports that the West Antarctic ice-sheet is melting. If it collapses the sea levels could rise more than 4.88 metres (16 feet). Both London and Bangladesh will be drowned. Meanwhile, American scientists now predict that the likelihood of the Gulf Stream 'pump' switching off due to excessive meltwater in the Arctic is greater than 50%. And the glaciers in the Himalayas that ensure the annual flow for the river systems of the Indian subcontinent and Southeast Asia? Retreating. Without the irrigation they provide, 1 billion people will be displaced. Then there are the matters of $CO_2$ dissolving in the oceans, acidifying the seas and making them virtually uninhabitable; a 1°C rise in temperature making tropical rainforests unviable; and a 1-2°C rise making trout disappear from the Rockies. Even if we stopped all emissions now there is still likely to be a 0.6°C rise because the effects of climate change happen over decades, not years. The grimmest prediction is that there will be a 90% die off of the global human population. I could go on but just search the web (Michael McCarthy, *Independent* newspaper, IPCC). It is all there.

Let's try to put this into some perspective*: Annual world military expenditure is $780 billion. To eradicate famine and implement sustainable agriculture would cost $17 billion per year for ten years – just 32% of what the US spends on candy every year. To implement renewable energy? Another $17 billion per year for ten years – 13% of current subsidies to electricity prices in the developing world or 2.2% of the world's annual military budget. To reverse deforestation? If we planted 150 million hectares in the next decade, it would cost $6 billion a year. Add another billion for rainforest protection and financial incentives and that is just 0.9% of the world's

* Statistics from: www.worldgame.org

total annual military expenditure. Can we do it? We already have a model … Just $300 million eradicated smallpox by 1978. This interests me because our problems aren't about money – they are about mindsets. It is tempting to wring our collective hands in shame and feel utterly overwhelmed by the scale of the pending disaster and the sheer madness of our current levels of consumption, but we can't afford to. We cannot avert change but it does offer us an unparalleled opportunity to transform our relationship with planet Earth and therefore ourselves. This is our challenge and one we can all choose to accept.

At *PM*, we have consequently entered a period of greater focus. We will continue to report on a wide array of sustainable, low carbon methods of gardening, agriculture, building and technology from all over the world. We will print unflinching facts about climate change, Peak Oil and the shape of our collective future, but we want to find ways of altering this powerless mindset. We will explore ways of working together and creating networks of mutual support to enable us to be more effective, spread our message and live more ecologically. Added to this, we intend to report back to you on personal strategies for staying motivated, empowered and sane in a world in crisis. In other words, we will do all we can as editors, publishers and activists to supply useful material, best practice, inspiration and support. We ask you to stay engaged. It is natural to feel depression and despair about the future, but if we continue to educate ourselves, gain new skills, adapt and champion alternatives to this dying post-industrial world, new undreamed of possibilities will emerge and we will find them. We owe it to the beings of the future to do so.

# 45 | Autumn 2005

Last May, I heard Joanna Macy, the American deep ecologist and activist, speak in Oxford. She campaigned on various vital issues from the sixties onwards in reactionary America: nuclear disarmament, the Vietnam War, the conservation of rainforests and indiscriminate logging of old growth forests … and now, in the autumn of her life, she has started campaigning for political, economic and scientific accountability for climate change and Peak Oil. At one point in the evening, she spoke about her friend and fellow founder of the deep ecology movement, John Seed. She described him standing in front of a hostile crowd of loggers with bulldozers in an Australian rainforest, determined to prevent logging. Suddenly, he had an epiphany. He realised that he was not just one small individual protester. He was the rainforest. He was the Lifeforce of this beautiful, biodiverse and irreplaceable sanctuary and he was the intimate web of life that flowed through the landscape. The rainforest took the shape of his body; it flowed through him, within him, throughout him. There was no question of not standing there and facing the angry crowds and the bulldozers and he did it with equanimity, in a state of peace, realisation and love. And he was literally immoveable. He could 'think like a mountain' and that force transformed his physical body as well as the power of his intentions. He later wrote, "There and then I was gripped with an intense, profound realisation of the depth of the bonds that connect us to the Earth, how deep are our feelings for these connections. I knew then that I was no longer acting on behalf of myself or my human ideas, but on behalf of the Earth … on behalf of my larger self, that I was literally part of the rainforest defending herself."*

This to me is the essence of deep ecology: to realise our oneness with the web of life – not just as an intellectual understanding of systems science or applied ecology – but as knowledge, consciousness … This is real power. There is no force on Earth greater than this consciousness. It is beyond the personal, not driven by the personality but fired by a deeper connection with the Self. Our personal philosophies will define this Self according to our beliefs, but whatever we call it, when we have this consciousness we become a part of universality, which can be characterised by peace and harmlessness. Joanna's story and my subsequent meeting with her (see this issue) made a deep impression on me. I started to see how we can really face the challenges of this century and maintain our enthusiasm, our humour and our love of life without denying the realities around us. Above all, we can be powerful yet at peace.

We live in a time of terrible violence. During the G8 I watched balaclavaed so-called 'ecoactivists' smashing in police windscreens. I wondered how many peaceful protesters were there, attempting to put their message across, largely ignored by the press and blockaded into camps by

---

* *Thinking Like a Mountain*, John Seed *et al*, New Society, p.8. Sadly out of print.

the police. It must have been tough being sandwiched between police and a violent anarchic element. It is not that I am beyond anger myself. I can understand rage at our leaders who have forced our national involvement in the Iraq War with its proliferation of low grade uranium weapons and other atrocities. I can be angry at the 'system' that manipulates aid, demanding conditional procurement and wields subsidies like weapons, blocking fair trade and a decent price for commodities. I can feel impotently angry about our dysfunctional culture whose values seem so selfish and skewed. And though I could never condone terrorism, I can understand how we have arrived at the door of suicide bombing in Britain. The escalation of British aggression in the Middle East has invited this awful symptom of impotent rage. I cannot begin to imagine the horror of being bombed and crawling out of the underground, nor the terrible grief of losing a friend or relative. My heart goes out to the bereaved and I feel compassion for the British Muslim community. I also feel compassion for those who feel driven to such extreme acts of violence, and to their stunned families. Yet these events bring a clarity. We have no choice but to deconstruct this culture which threatens the ecosystems of the planet and our very survival, but we cannot deconstruct it with violence and rage. That will only fuel the current paradigm. We have to painstakingly deconstruct whilst holding a vision of a peaceful future, when the basis for civilisation is founded on harmlessness, harmlessness to each other, harmlessness to the ecosystems, harmlessness to the planet. This isn't wishy-washy middle-class liberalism; it is the path of our collective survival.

*In the depth of winter I finally learned that there was in me an invincible summer.*

Albert Camus

A good existential beginning! This quote explores the metaphor of transition. The human race faces unprecedented challenges of adaptation – to escalating climate change and energy descent in the form of Peak Oil. These two human-induced catastrophes spell a bleak future. Already climate change is affecting hundreds of thousands of people across the globe – more hurricanes, floods, landslides, droughts, forest fires – and the rises in energy costs are impacting on the global economy, in areas such as transport, manufacturing, and retailing. Inevitably, it is the world's poor who are most vulnerable. But I am not going to explore the social inequity of energy descent or the critical impact of climate change – there is enough gloomy news – I want to focus on an energy debate that is at the core of resistance to positive social transition.

The anti-windpower lobby in the UK for instance is quite astonishing. I often hear what is pure propaganda given as statements of fact. Let me list some of them. 'Wind turbines kill birds.' Only if you are idiot enough to site a turbine on a migratory route. 'Windpower is unreliable.' When we have increased demand in the UK (like for that post-FA Cup Final cup of tea) Sizewell B nuclear plant trips out. It is no more reliable. 'Windpower is noisy.' Go to Swaffham in Norfolk and listen to the turbine. It's in a residential area and the residents are not complaining. 'In order to satisfy UK demand you would need to site turbines all the way around our coastline.' This statement does not take account of the potential for other sources of renewable energy – no micro-hydro, no tidal, no combined heat and power biomass, no domestic-scale turbines and no photovoltaics. It assumes that we introduce no energy conservation measures at all and that the whole energy system is run as 'business as usual' – and that we just go on consuming energy at our current profligate rate.

I am not pretending that energy descent planning will be easy or will not require deep social change, but I do think that the anti-wind, pro 'clean' coal (no such thing), nuclear lobby is symptomatic of a fantasy to maintain the failing status quo. This strategy conveniently ignores the fact we have no adequate ways to dispose of spent nuclear fuel, deal with terrorist attacks on nuclear power plants or stop the escalation of nuclear weapons in countries that do not buy into our Western hegemony. It ignores the energy costs of extracting oil from shale and hopes for the unlikely event of a technological magic bullet. Furthermore, the idea of local and regional self-reliance is outside the mindset of the many who are frankly hypnotised by the centralised industrial paradigm and who want to keep it that way – a narrow vision of 'Command and Control' which I believe to be deeply uncreative and dangerous.

To return to Camus' winter and our invincible summer. We are on the brink of a systems breakdown. The old ways are simply not sustainable, not for us now or for any generation to come. Our present culture is bringing a metaphoric as well as possibly a literal winter of such severity and suffering that **we have to change**. So what can we do? We need to face reality and see these challenges as opportunities. Whilst studying Peak Oil and watching the world's news, I have been imagining a different future: one in which most city trees are edible species; where the majority of rural and urban land is given to growing food and fuel; where areas of wilderness are honoured and protected; where human and animal waste is converted into fertile soil; where small-scale horticulture and agriculture is no longer the work of a marginalised peasantry but part of a movement for intelligent self-reliance; where every town and village has a portfolio of individual and community renewable energy systems and a local economy; where every settlement is retrofitted for energy conservation; where every new build meets stringent ecological standards; where every community resource is designed in relation to meeting the needs of its people; where every resource possible is renewed before it is considered for recycling. This to me is not a wintery world of scarcity and energy poverty; it is a world of diversity, self-reliance, real wealth and satisfying creativity.

*History reveals that when humanity is faced with new challenges that cannot be solved with old thinking, new capacities at mental and biological levels will evolve. We are now living in a point in history when changing life conditions are of such magnitude that a new worldview with a transformative vision is beginning to emerge.*

NANCY ROOF
co-founder,
United Nations Values Caucus

I have been casting my mind back to when I first started writing editorials in the mid-nineties. In those days, my subject was often an explanation of permaculture design and why it was a good thing. Many greens at that time knew little about it, let alone the mainstream, and it was generally regarded as a dubious Australian invention unsuitable for export to cool temperate and other climatic adaptations. Time, and the work of authors like Patrick Whitefield, have relieved many of this misconception.

Then, as I warmed to my job, I began beating the drum of environmental awareness, exhorting readers to sit up and take note of the reality of climate change, dwindling resources and biodiversity, the threatened fate of the Gulf Stream, Peak Oil … I was playing my part in trying to engage people in the process of changing their beliefs and lifestyles. Increasingly today, mainstream television and newspapers inform millions of people who want to hear. The science of climate change, our ecological planetary crisis and Peak Oil are accepted facts, even to the reluctant

White House. We are not short of reliable information.

Despite this, the challenge for many is twofold. Firstly, we know what's going on in the wider world is true, but what can we do about it? The problems are huge and we can think it's up to governments to find solutions, not individuals. Secondly, even if we accept that we can make the small changes that collectively change the world, the news is so grim, what is the point? We're all gonna die anyway! The very fact that you are reading this magazine means you do not fall into category one. You are already aware of the crisis and the need to respond, but you may just feel the hopelessness of the situation and fall into category two. Given the enormity of our problems, this is a very sane response. I do … sometimes. So how do we stay engaged in the face of catastrophic information like the consequence of Greenland melting in the near future? How do we keep on walking our talk and maintaining a sense of commitment and optimism, despite the timescale of reversing climate change *et al*?

Besides my job, I have a number of personal strategies to stay engaged. Firstly, I 'follow my joy'. This involves appreciating simple pleasures like sunsets and sunrises, seeds germinating, warm fires and good books, beautiful scenery, long walks, friends and my dear family. None of them cost money. I am not a great consumer. I don't give a damn about what car I drive (though I appreciate energy efficiency and well designed machines and tools). I find the deliberate obsolescence of designer clothes totally irritating. My friends know I love charity (aka thrift) shops.

Secondly, I remind myself that life can be totally unpredictable. I am old enough to remember the tanks rolling into Prague in 1968. As a little girl I heard the news on the radio and felt the fear. Later on, I could never have predicted the sudden collapse of the Berlin Wall and the Soviet Union nor the triumph of Nelson Mandela and the establishment of a free South Africa. This tells me that however dark our future may be, we cannot predict it in its entirety. It is therefore necessary to try and live this life in the moment and not allow ourselves to project our fears on to a future we don't yet know. This is not denial – we still have to act – it is an acknowledgement that marvellous, unexpected triumphs are possible. We humans are capable of fundamentally changing our worldviews and therefore our relationships with each other.

A poignant way in which I have been learning the art of living in the moment is from my elderly mother. Last year she had a stroke that has affected her memory. Remembering what she has done five minutes ago, let alone yesterday or last year, is difficult, sometimes impossible. Instead of being self-pitying and defeated, however, she has adapted to her situation with courage and magnanimity. The fact is that often there is only 'the moment' for her and this has made her joyful and appreciative of each day she has left. No longer able to drive a car, she tells me that she uses her empty garage as a place to dance.

*Permaculture offers a radical approach to food production and urban renewal, water, energy and pollution. It integrates ecology, landscape design, organic gardening, architecture and agroforestry in creating a rich and sustainable way of living. It uses appropriate technology giving high yields for low energy inputs, achieving a resource of great diversity and stability. The design principles are equally applicable to urban and rural dwellers.*

BILL MOLLISON

Bill Mollison, the co-originator of perma-culture and its Grand Old Man, so succinctly sums up the huge breadth of permaculture.

Permaculture isn't a method of gardening, forestry or building. It is a way of thinking and organising – it is intelligent ecological and ethical design. It does not focus on the elements of sustainability in themselves – the detail of organics, ecobuilding, appropriate technology, community building – permaculture looks at the *beneficial relationships between the elements* and how they are put together to make them as energy efficient and sustaining as possible, both for the planet and all its ecosystems – and this includes its people. After all, we are part of Nature as much as any other element; we have just forgotten this. Permaculture enhances our observation and understanding of natural patterns and universal principles. It teaches us to contemplate Nature and natural systems and then to apply these 'ecological truisms' to our own circumstances.

Now, this all sounds rather technical and specialised (and maybe even a little

mystical!) … We live in a world of experts in which 'design' is the preserve of profes-sionals who we are encouraged to consult before taking decisions or actions. We even have garden designers on tap, too complex are our little plots to risk amateur interven-tion. But permaculture's greatest strength and inspiration is that it isn't a set of rules or rigid principles to be obeyed – it is a way of opening the mind, inspiring the spirit and harnessing our own creativity so that we can take control of our lives and do things for ourselves.

Crucial also is permaculture's educa-tional aspect. This is not a dry intellectual exercise, judged on the absorption of facts, but an eye opening, practical, experiential process that is part of the internationally taught Permaculture Design Course. This course helps us to recognise and develop our individual skills, confidence and imagination so we can become more self-reliant. This doesn't mean that we all have to become self-sufficient. What is essential to individual self-reliance is not doing everything ourselves but the establishment of beneficial relationships within our local community. Whilst one person grows food, another builds ecohouses, another manages woodlands, and another publishes useful information, or installs renewable energy systems or develops sustainable forests or farms (or even forest farms!). We are all different and we can celebrate this diversity by creating self-reliant local community networks and economies.

Over the course of the last 16 years since I discovered permaculture, I have had the privilege to meet many creative, intelligent people. I recently spent the weekend with Ben Law at his woodland, a place I have had the good fortune to return to over the years. I have seen his Woodland House and its gardens maturing among the trees, the restoration of the derelict coppice that lies beyond his boundaries, and have witnessed Ben's unquenchable appetite to leave the landscape that surrounds him in better ecological health than he found it. Last month, at a Permaculture Association meeting in Oxford, I met people who are working in the poorest areas of urban deprivation with very few resources, creating food and flower gardens, cleaning up syringe-ridden derelict lots, inspiring young children who have never played in woodlands before to learn crafts, encouraging those who have fallen victim to mental illness or homelessness to socialise, grow food, learn new skills … It is people like this who put permaculture into practice and inspire others to do the same. They raise my spirits and give me heart for the future, however it is going to unfold. They demonstrate that we all have the potential and creative imagination to become more self-reliant, even in the most difficult of circumstances, and ultimately to leave this Earth a better place than when we found it.

It seems we are edging towards a brave new world in the UK – or should I say resurrection of the insane old worldview that nuclear power is a viable option. The current government's own White Paper in 2003 recommended that the nuclear option was too expensive. The recent New Economic Foundation's research confirmed that nuclear energy is very far from carbon neutral in terms of building, operating and decommissioning plants, let alone disposing of the waste. So why are we still pursuing this unholy grail?

I have recently spent some time with a former US environmental scientist, Dr Will Keeping. He was part of an energy project to calculate whether the U.S. could satisfy its energy requirements (without any conservation measures) with renewables. The answer was a resounding 'yes' – easily – the US is such an incredibly resource rich country in terms of wind, sun, water and tides! He also told me about the time he worked for international think tanks researching and developing renewable and photovoltaic technologies. It became obvious to him that micro-renewables (small-scale, home- or community-based energy production) could become a force for good and help combat poverty and disease. They could be used to pump clean water to remote villages, make education available through improved communications, to power hospitals and so on. The World Bank was persuaded to fund photovoltaic programmes to aid 'development' in various so-called Third World countries. But what did they fund? Not the clean water pumps or the educational programmes, but the installation of small satellite dishes in remote areas so that commercial US television could be beamed in, promoting all the values associated with consumerism and the Western lifestyle, undermining traditional indigenous culture. They proved that it is possible to use 'appropriate' technology totally inappropriately. Will resigned from his job. He says that unless we have the right values, it doesn't matter what tools, technology and resources we develop. He now devotes his life to understanding how we can affect a shift in our cultural values and he helps individuals to make those changes on a personal level. I wish Tony Blair would take his counsel.

This morning Starhawk, US author, activist and permaculturist, told me the story of the Diablo Cannon nuclear plant in central California which was built on an earthquake fault. Work started in the late 1970s amid a huge anti-nuclear resistance campaign against the plant. This culminated in a massive non-violent blockade in 1981 when five thousand people were arrested. At the end of the blockade an engineer working at the plant revealed that the two reactors built next to one another were not exact copies of each other, but mirror images. The construction workers had mixed up the blueprints and built parts of each reactor back to front. It took the utility company, Pacific Gas and Electric, a further three years to rebuild the reactors. The plant went on line in 1984 but it proved so costly to commission due to delays caused by the blockade and mistakes in construction that the company cancelled plans for all further reactors in California. Completing the plant was therefore a pyrrhic victory for the company. It also had an incalculable positive effect on the protest movement in the US which had learned how to set up affinity groups, develop models for non-violent protest and consensus, and went on to become effective in organising campaigns against nuclear weapons, military interventions and global injustice.

Despite the potential of micro-generation, our government still thinks of renewables in terms of large-scale projects such as wind farms and hydro-electric plants. Micro-renewables could account for 40% of our energy, but the funding to encourage development and installation is pitiful. Secondly, there is no serious conservation programme for energy – or any real attempt to affect a shift in public values – it is clearly business as usual in government. The idea that the nuclear power business will be privately funded is untrue. The nuclear lobby will attract millions in government funding (and billions for decommissioning) and the carbon saved using this lethal technology is highly debatable. I do not believe there is a political mandate for starting another nuclear programme. I am personally of the opinion that we need to learn from the American activists, hone our non-violent protest skills and stop this ecological madness.

I never imagined, when Tim and I started this magazine in 1992, that we would reach issue 50. At that time my concept of permaculture was very different to what it is today.

I saw it as an intelligent design system for growing food, generating power, ecobuilding, woodland management … a system of greater self-reliance that was by its nature outside mainstream society and in those days, dare I say, rather elitist. And I saw myself as a person who had always found herself on the edge as well, rejecting the values of materialism and overconsumption, celebrating organic resources and finding food for free. I had a lot to learn.

It's a very different world today. Although our governments seem paralysed by climate change, Peak Oil and the collapse of societies where Western 'democracy' has been enforced upon them, there is a profound awakening occurring. We know we are in trouble and that we have to cut carbon emissions and rebuild the way society works. We even know what to do and how to legislate in the UK. Friends of the Earth, the Co-operative Bank and the Tyndall Centre for Climate Change have just summarised extensive research in a report called *The Future Starts Here: The Route to a Low-Carbon Economy*. It offers strategies to reduce emissions and calls for a policy and legislative framework for Britain to do so. It says we must 'stay put' below a 2°C increase in global temperature and tells us that "the way we live daily life does not need to be radically different in a low-carbon economy. We will have warm houses … leisure and mobility. What will change radically is how energy efficient our lives are, and where we get our energy from."

I welcome this report and its framework. But by itself, I doubt that this is enough for us to realistically hit the 'below 2°C' ceiling on global temperatures by 2030. September 2006 in Britain was already the hottest on record with the temperature 3.2°C higher than average. I think we are well on our way to busting the 2°C threshold and beyond. It's a grim scenario.

More than energy conservation and new technologies, there needs to be a radical shift in our worldview, from unchecked consumption of resources to Earth Stewardship. This requires a massive cut in carbon emission, a relocalisation of our food supply and economy, and most critically of all, an engagement and mobilisation of the whole population in the realities of living in an interdependent planetary system with finite resources. This is where permaculture circa 2006 comes in. Permaculture is not only about designing individual 'lifeboats' to protect us from climate chaos. It is part of an evolving box of tools that can be used to engage people in redesigning their entire communities. This is much more exciting and expansive than ecohomesteading. Our challenge is to engage with our wider community, both urban and rural, change the way we live so that we do have a future and to truly integrate the ethics of earth care, people care and fair shares that underpin permaculture philosophy. We have to do this for future generations and for this beautiful planet Earth and all her surviving species. We therefore lead *PM*50 with Rob Hopkins' article about how to inspire communities to adopt low carbon transition strategies. Since Rob wrote this article, there are now meetings for fledgling Transition Towns in Falmouth and Penzance. Let's hope the idea goes to every town hall in this country and beyond. Then we will have the political mandate to insist that government adopt the policies of the FoE report and more.

When I look back over 50 issues of *PM*, I can feel nothing but gratitude for being involved in this magazine. It has been a steep learning curve for Tim and me personally and a privilege to feel we are doing a job that is life-enhancing and positive, even though it has been a great struggle to keep it going at times. So I would like to extend our gratitude to all the writers who educate and inspire us; gratitude to our faithful editors who lend their various perspectives and expertise to every issue; gratitude to the team here at Permanent Publications who steer, design, pack and dispatch each issue together and help keep the whole adventure rolling; gratitude to our advertisers, distributors and suppliers; but above all, gratitude to all our readers who keep the vision alive and make publishing it possible. Maybe we are still on the pioneering edge, exploring new ideas and impatiently waiting for the mainstream to catch up, but I personally still wouldn't be anywhere else.

" I understand above all hope as a state of mind, not a state of the world. Either we have hope within us, or we don't … Hope is not prognostication. It is an orientation of the spirit, an orientation of the heart. It transcends the world that is immediately experienced, and is anchored somewhere beyond its horizons … Hope is not the same thing as optimism. It is not the conviction that something will turn out well, but the certainty that something makes sense, regardless of how it turns out … this hope … gives us the strength to live and continually to try new things, even in conditions that seem as hopeless as ours do, here and now.

Vaclav Havel
*Disturbing the Peace*, pp.181-182

# Section Three

# 2007 - 2009

World population is 6.613 billion.

**6 August 2007**, President Ramos-Horta names independence activist Xanana Gusmão as prime minister of East Timor.

**26 September 2007**, after a month of peaceful pro-democracy demonstrations that include hundreds of monks, Burmese government forces shoot at crowds. Dozens of people are killed.

**28 October 2007**, Cristina Fernández de Kirchner is elected Argentina's first woman president. She succeeds her husband, Néstor Kirchner.

**3 December 2007**, US National Intelligence Estimates says 'with high confidence' that Iran froze its nuclear weapons program in 2003. The report contradicts one written in 2005 that stated Iran was determined to continue developing such weapons.

**19 February 2008**, Cuban president Fidel Castro, who temporarily handed power to his brother Raúl in July 2006 when he fell ill, permanently steps down after 49 years in power.

**11 March 2008**, the US government begins to intervene in the financial system to avoid a crisis. The Federal Reserve outlines a $200 billion loan programme that lets the country's biggest banks borrow Treasury securities at discounted rates and post mortgage-backed securities as collateral.

**22 August 2008**, as many as 90 Afghan civilians, 60 of them children, die in an airstrike by coalition troops in the western village of Azizabad.

**5 November 2008**, Barack Obama is elected the first African-American president of the US.

**7 Feb 2009**, the worst wildfires in Australia's history kill at least 181 people.

**1 April 2009**, Sweden becomes the fifth European country to legalize same-sex marriage. The other countries with the same rights are The Netherlands, Norway, Belgium and Spain.

**26 April 2009**, H1N1 (swine flu) has killed as many as 103 people in Mexico, most likely the epicentre of the worldwide outbreak.

In the permaculture world, the *New Internationalist* devoted an entire issue to permaculture and I contributed to it. It felt like a breakthrough that another magazine was exploring the subject in depth.

Geoff Lawton released a film, *Harvesting Water, the Permaculture Way*.

Eric Toensmeier's book, *Perennial Vegetables*, was published by Chelsea Green.

On 20-25 March 2008, the movement celebrated its 30th birthday with an Australian Permaculture Convergence. Permaculture's two founders were in attendance with a host of other luminaries, including Geoff Lawton (Permaculture Research Institute), Max Lindegger (Ecological Solutions), Josh Byrnes (Gardening Australia), Michael Mobbs (The Sustainable House), Robyn Francis (Erda Institute), Rosemary Morrow (*Earth User's Guide to Permaculture*), and the Cuban activist, Roberto Perez.

In November of 2009, Malawi in Central Africa hosted the International Permaculture Convergence (IPC9). Almost 150 people from close to 50 different countries gathered and the Malawi government sent Dr. Mary Shawa, the Principal Secretary from the Office of the President and Cabinet (OPC) and the head of the Department of Nutrition and HIV to address the delegates. She emphasised the importance of using local resources in meeting the challenges of food security, ending malnutrition, and disease prevention as well as treatment.

In 2007, Permanent Publications published *Do It Yourself 12 Volt Solar Power* by Michel Daniek which has now sold over 10,000 copies. Also published that year were the first of the Four Keys to Sustainability series, endorsed by UNESCO, *Beyond You and Me: Inspirations and Wisdom for Building Community* edited by Kosha Anja Joubert & Robin Alfred, *The Woodland Year* by Ben Law (2008) and *The Living Landscape* by Patrick Whitefield (2009).

During this time Permanent Publications received a number of awards for best practice as an ecobusiness, the most notable being a Queen's Award for Enterprise in 2008 for our "unfettered dedication to promoting sustainable development internationally". It felt like a watershed for permaculture.

In 2009, Rebecca Hosking and Tim Green made an hour long TV programme for the BBC's Natural History Unit, 'A Farm For the Future', exploring how Peak Oil will affect farming and food distribution and why permaculture design and other regenerative agriculture practices could be a solution. Millions of people watched the first screening – so much so that the BBC re-screened the film within weeks. It was the first time permaculture was presented seriously in mainstream media.

In the Harlands' world, our eldest daughter has completed school and is now studying music. Our youngest is studying Art at college. Both are still living at home but we feel their wings beating! Tim and I reach the landmark of 50 years old. Tim hadn't taken a long haul flight in decades, me only one on Gaia Education business. We had all but given up flying, influenced by Patrick Whitefield, who said there was never any justification for the carbon expended in a single flight. But our wings were also beating, having been publishing without a break since 1990, and producing the magazine since 1992. One morning, drinking tea in bed, Tim said, "I would love to go to Bhutan." I said, to his great surprise, "OK. Let's go!" In 2008 there was to be a total solar eclipse in the Himalayas. We flew to Kathmandu, Nepal and visited Buddhist and Hindu UNESCO World Heritage Sites. To this day, I have the serene face of the standing Buddha there on my laptop screen. It is a statue of exquisite beauty. I hope it survived the terrible earthquake that was to later devastate Nepal.

Then we took a flight to Bhutan, landing almost blind as the small airfield is accessed by flying around a mountain. Only three pilots in the world are qualified to fly this route. Bhutan was full of memorable experiences. Standing high

on a Himalayan mountain we watched the solar eclipse.
We also climbed to 10,000 feet to the Tiger's Nest,
a monastery on the site where Guru Rinpoche 'rode the
tiger's back' to enlightenment and founded Buddhism in
Bhutan. We visited dzongs (monastic, military, administrative
and social centres), encountered the story of the Divine
Madman, and explored the Bhutanese centre for traditional
medicine. In Thimpu, the capital city (very modest in size),
we met a Bhutanese football fan who told us a number of
facts we didn't know about Portsmouth FC, our local club in
England. We saw the extraordinary confluence of a society
firmly rooted in, and controlled by, tradition and spiritual
and royal hierarchy, and the pervasive influence of the secular
West. Tim took a picture of a satellite dish placed on the stump
of a vast, ancient tree. It seem to sum up the challenges.
Retrospectively, I think the trip did us good. It was an
adventure, a cultural education, and it took us out of our
rather small lives and reminded us both of the great, big
world out there with all its complexities, poverty and rich
cultural diversity.

# 51 | Spring 2007

This is in every sense a new beginning for *PM*, the first issue beyond our half century and one which will reach more people than ever before. Not only have we finally reached the shelves of high street newsagents in the UK after years of discussion, we will also be seen in countries as far afield as Australia and Taiwan (see 'News' in this issue). This is humbling. It seems no coincidence then that I write this in England as winter moves into spring, a time the Celts traditionally celebrated the re-emerging lifeforce and the opportunity for new beginnings. Like the Celts, we can set our intentions for what we want to grow, plant the seeds of new beginnings, make conscious choices and start to set them in motion.

Last year, one of Tim's and my chosen 'seeds' was that we would attend the Climate Change March in London in November. We wanted to be counted. It was a real community affair, meeting friends on the train on the way there and during the event, and though the speeches were fiery, it was a peaceful, good humoured day. There was something wonderful about walking through the West End of London, closed to traffic, enjoying the space, the people and the architecture. I highly recommend this annual event which brings into focus, not only our fate if we don't change the way we live, but also a genuine concern for the wellbeing of the planet and all of its people, especially in the countries who will suffer most. My regret is that only 25,000 people attended and therefore the media and politicians were able to dismiss the event with ease. It feels

good to be counted, but we need to be counted in our millions. Please join us next year. It's a global event on your doorstep.

As individuals we have the power to change our lives by our actions, and that our personal actions have tiny but incremental effects on others. There are many stories of what we can do in our homes, gardens and the wider community to reduce our carbon footprint. These represent a world that is less selfish, less greedy for 'things', more creative … a world in which people connect with each other, with the soil, and with their hands through inspiring, practical projects. This is the essence of permaculture: applied positive vision.

Our future is created by the choices we make now, and the more positive the choices we make the more we alter the collective consciousness. There is an emerging shift in the world – a growing concern for our planet and its people – and we all have a significant opportunity to encourage and support this change. Has Joanna Macy's Great Turning already begun? (www.joannamacy.net) I hope so. The more people feel hope, the more likely they will be to apply the positive vision that will make the difference. Author, Glennie Kindred, speaks of us all adding to the collective consciousness to influence our future not just by our actions, but by our very thoughts and conversations.

We can all play our part in creating the future. This is not a future wherein we lose the plot and fail to cut global carbon emission. This is a future in which we awaken to our personal and global responsibility

– a true maturation of humanity from adolescence into adulthood. It's easy to feel the burden of climate change and think that it's too austere, or even impossible for us to reduce carbon consumption adequately. This attitude is as unacceptable as noisily partying the night away whilst a neighbour lies dying. So whilst we invite and celebrate new beginnings into our lives and renew our hope, let's also invite greater collective awareness. Dr Jeremy Leggett (www.solarcentury.co.uk) talks about climate change being one of the 'great oversights of our time'. It is an issue so important that we should be taking to the streets, yet in the 'over-developed' world we mostly sit on our hands, waiting for others to act first. Al Gore made a pertinent observation in the film, 'An Inconvenient Truth'. He said that ignoring climate change is like the policy of appeasement in the 1930s. Nations ignored the growth of fascism, hoping that it would be contained by national boundaries and not trouble them. We have been mainly ignoring climate change since the early 1990s when the IPCC panel of scientists first met. Following their meeting this February in Paris, perhaps at last, with a broad scientific consensus that climate change is a reality and caused by human activity, this will curtail our ignorance and finally galvanise our governments and industry into action. We, and an increasing number of people all over the world, however, are not waiting for governments or industry to act, we are acting already – and that's what permaculture is all about.

A part of my work is to watch ecofilms and keep abreast of events. I watched Al Gore's film, 'An Inconvenient Truth', at home alone on an early release DVD some months ago. Whatever you think of Al Gore or his proffered technological- and business-led solutions to climate change, he offers a clear and eloquent plea for immediate carbon reduction and his film has reached millions. Everyone should see it. My first viewing had me shedding private tears for the state of our planet and for the millions of people who will be affected by inevitable global warming. (I do shed tears and I know I am not alone. It is a healthy response to our predicament.) The second time I watched the film was with my daughter at a free viewing which was part of the launch of a campaign to green our local town, Petersfield. At the end of the film I watched people file out in shock. The local populace, like millions across the world, had no idea how suicidal unchecked climate change is. In that shock is a dangerous set of potential symptoms of feelings of personal despair and disempowerment – that it may be too big, too difficult, too late to do anything to make a difference. The second thing that hit me that evening is that we must keep on talking about the solutions.

Sabine Lichtenfels is a peace activist in the Middle East and a co-founder of the Tamera Peace Research Village in Portugal. Tamera is a research settlement where the important themes of a new, sustainable culture are being developed. For the last 27 years Sabine has been working together with a sociologist, Dieter Duhm, to create a peaceful, ecologically balanced community and restore the landscape around them. The community embodies the concept that "those who don't want war need a vision for peace". Sabine also restores 'inner' landscapes and a main focus of her political work is training youth and peace work in the Middle East.

Two years ago, together with the students of the Peace School Mirja, she put on the theatre piece called 'We Refuse To Be Enemies' based on the most moving stories and statements from the peace camps and then toured Europe with it. So why am I telling you these stories?

As climate change escalates we will hear more and more 'bad' news in newspapers, on TV, in apocalyptic films. Although this will wake up the ecologically asleep, it is currently only defining what is wrong and being sketchy about how to put it right. Yet we cannot create a new world by only fighting the old. This results in an exhausting and negative vacuum and feelings of despair and disempowerment. We need to build our visions and put them into practice piece by piece, garden by garden, community by community, city by city. We are literally seeding the future.

Permaculture – along with the work of Joanna Macy and the peace workers of Tamera and others – has been practising the practical application of positive visions for over 30 years. Permaculture has a track record of designing abundant, low impact systems and offering solutions. Like the peace workers, however, we have to be resolute. Just as Palestinians and Israelis can refuse to be enemies, we can refuse to be daunted and derailed by the impending catastrophe of climate change, and the best way to do this is by finding kindred spirits. It is an 'old' political idea that the grassroots cannot make a significant difference, that all change must be led from the top down. I like the quote by John Page at the beginning of the Brazilian film, 'A Convenient Truth': "I can't understand why people are frightened of new ideas. I'm frightened of the old ones."

This year, more rain fell in 24 hours across Britain than usually falls in the entire month of June and the flood water has damaged an estimated 31,200 homes and 7,000 businesses. UK insurers are facing a bill of about £1.5bn. Meanwhile, the western USA is suffering a multi-year drought with extreme risk of wildfire. Chicago and Miami are regularly hitting temperatures in the '90s (F). I sat on a panel at Reading University recently and Dr Brenda Boardman, programme leader of Lower Carbon Futures at Oxford University, revealed that scientists now believe that we only have a window of four years to radically reduce carbon. After that, we are pretty much toast. I find that chilling. She also said that we must focus on solutions, not get weighed down by the enormity of the problem. The danger is that too much education as well as ignorance can tempt us to do nothing. Permaculture is all about integrated, holistic solutions.

In *PM46*, we published an article 'After the Flood, the Permaculture', about a West Yorkshire community's grassroots response to disastrous flooding in the Upper Calder Valley. To summarise, a combination of modern housing developments on flood plains; overgrazing and ploughing on sloping land, causing soil to be washed down and silt up flood defences; the loss or damage to ecosystems like woodlands, swamps, marshes and bogs that work like sponges to soak up excess water; plus more rain (a month's average in a day, for example) and storms symptomatic of climate change, make more floods inevitable.

The permaculture response was to start reforesting the valley close to the watershed – an urgent necessity to minimise the run-off. The idea is to keep the water on the Pennine hills for as long as possible. Local people may not be able to control building on flood plains or the destruction of marsh habitats immediately but we can plant trees. To date, Treesponsibility (www.treesponsibility.com), the grassroots organisation involved, have planted thousands of trees on land made available by local farmers.

Curitiba, a city in Brazil with two million inhabitants, is another example. The city suffered annual flooding which mainly hit its poor who lived in slums on marginal land. The city government paid their residents to move out of the slums into affordable housing, served by an integrated transport system, business and social enterprise schemes and schools. They then turned their flood plain into a series of beautiful urban water parks with the capacity to absorb and direct floodwater away from the city. Tourism tripled. What the city council lacked in funds, they made up for in imagination and political will.

My point of course is that we can all act positively, whatever our resources or spheres of influence. One excuse, I often hear, for doing nothing is that India and China are rapidly industrialising: what's the point of the US or Europe cutting carbon emissions? The reality is that though China, for example, demonstrates the highest current growth rate in emissions, its emissions per person are still below the global average and its accumulated contribution since the start of the Industrial Revolution around 1800 is only five per cent of the global total. This compares to the US and Europe which have each contributed more than 25% of accumulated global emissions.*

* Dr Mike Raupach, co-Chair of the Global Carbon Project, CSIRO Marine and Atmospheric Research scientist, www.sciencealert.com.au/carbon-reduction-failing-5.html

In the past few weeks, Tim and I have joined with others to start a local Greening Campaign.* We are lucky in our work and play, and spend a lot of time with like-minded people, but we are always keen to do more at the grassroots. The point of the greening campaigns is to engage local people (who do not regard themselves as environmental activists but who are worried about the science of climate change and its escalating effects) in strategies to reduce their personal carbon footprint.

It starts at the most basic level, encouraging people to switch the washing machine down to 30°C, change to energy saving light bulbs, walk rather than drive short distances, turn down the heating, in fact all the little lifestyle changes the government is currently promoting. Now I know that any environmentalist worth his or her salt will say that recycling plastic bags, walking to work or growing veg is pointless if we take long haul flights, for example, and that carbon reduction isn't about lipservice or being seen to do the right thing – it's about the effects of our collective overall actions. In the industrialised North, we have to reduce carbon output by 90% in the next ten years to have any effect on our children's futures. The baby steps involving laundry, light bulbs and woolly jumpers aren't going to 'save' anything, let alone a planet. But that is not the point. It misses the point by an iceberg.

It's very early days, but the fundamental idea behind our greening campaign is precisely not to get a bunch of already informed greenies or carbon counting experts telling people what not to do. The point is to help set up local events in villages, towns and city neighbourhoods and facilitate completely open and participatory meetings in which the community can decide for itself what it wants to do. The subtext for many of the participants is the desire to move with their community towards a Transition Movement initiative (as in Totnes, Lewis, Brixton, London and Bristol, etc.).** But as Terena Plowright, who started the whole greening campaign concept in East Hampshire, is keen to point out: "If you want to involve the majority of a community in lifestyle changes, they have to be appear attainable." First steps first …

In East Hampshire, it has been interesting to see the early results (most campaigns are just starting or have only been running a few months). One village showed the Al Gore film, did all its pledges about light bulbs and so on, calculated the carbon saved, engaged a significant proportion of the population – including the local school, churches, businesses and other village groups – and then decided as its first project to fundraise for a £45,000 renewable energy system for the local school. They have raised half the money already. Our local town also has the beginnings of a number of initiatives, one being an

*   www.greening-campaign.co.uk
**  See 'Powerdown & Permaculture', *PM*50.

alternative Christmas event in December. Only businesses with local or environmental goods can sell their wares in the market square, and there will be a candle-lit (and probably wind-up LED torch!) procession plus an open stage for people and groups to offer entertainment to the town. The idea is to get the community together, support local farmers, growers, crafts people and green traders, engage people and have fun.

I know this can be seen as tokenist behaviour. One little jolly market town procession or a photovoltaic array in a school will not stop the inexorable progress of our melting ice caps. It's not meant to. What these campaigns are designed to do is find 'the worried' who don't know what to do and bring them together with the already committed, the socially engaged, and other ecopeople, not at a big green gathering or climate change march, but in their own neighbourhoods. The point is to identify people who want to make changes, find support, learn skills, and gain knowledge. This also identifies those who are willing to speak to their friends, neighbours, schools, shops and so on, and start encouraging others to get involved. This process inevitably involves learning new skills – like how to facilitate a participatory meeting, how to draw together a diverse population of people and groups and arrive at consensus – and critically builds local networks. These are the baby steps: the very beginning of the painful but urgently needed process of creating awareness, mobilising local communities, and encouraging and inspiring action. It is not a means in itself. No one is fooling themselves that changing light bulbs will reverse climate change. Yet watching and participating in all this, I frequently hear the question, "What comes after stage one of the greening? Can't we do a Transition Town?" Stage Two – creating low carbon, permaculturally designed communities – is already on the horizon.

# 55 | Spring 2008

Deep ecologists have a powerful antidote for despair. They try to look at time from a different perspective. In essence, time is not linear, but circular. Joanna Macy speaks about 'deep time' expressing what we experience when we step outside the shrinking time box in which our culture encloses us. In Western industrialised culture we are increasingly cut off from the past and the future in that square cage in which we race, like a hamster on a wheel at increasingly frenetic speeds. Joanna believes that our disconnection with past and future is a fundamental reason why we are destroying the Earth. What does it matter if we destroy the past when the value of ancestry, be it ancient woodland or forest or the wisdom learnt through generations of stewardship of the land, is no longer in our awareness? It also doesn't matter if our culture is actively destroying the future through its consumption, industry and agriculture, if the future too is not remotely within our awareness on that frantic spinning wheel. Moving beyond the shrinking time box of the present is therefore fundamental to our culture's healing. We will stop cancelling out the future.

I had a direct experience of this when facilitating a workshop about deep ecology and climate change based on the work of Joanna Macy. A dedicated climate change activist in the group was so immersed in the latest scientific climate research and its ecological and social impacts that she had not allowed herself to imagine a future, so pressing was the urgent need to keep going and be effective in her present work.

We took a journey, firstly to return to the past and appreciate all the good aspects of society that we may have unwittingly left behind and then to call upon our ancestors to lend support to us as people trying to find the right path in our complex world. Next was a journey into the future. This is not the future of failure and devastation. This is a future, in the 22nd century, when global culture has turned away from all the destructive practices that are pouring $CO_2$ in the atmosphere, carbonising our rising seas, eradicating our ecological webs. This future is a post-industrial, ecological society, full of ingenious designs, creatively applied, with sensitive resource use and abundant landscapes. The journey deeply touched my activist friend because she had an insight into how she could climb out of her frantic little time box and draw strength and inspiration from the possibility of a future as yet fully unimagined but pervasively tangible in her consciousness. This nascent state is rather like awaking from a dream. The awareness of the dream is still present but clarity slides beyond conscious recall.

I have experienced this journey into a post-climate change future with a number of groups and every person's perception is naturally different. Yet the 'quality' of that future seems to have common threads. There is a sense of culture with greater inner resources. We are not wrapped in little boxes of our own making cut off from the lessons of the past and the potential of the future. There is also a great sense of peace and resolution, of a people who have

survived and moved beyond the warring
culture we are currently floundering in.
And naturally, for me, this is a society
bearing the marks of intelligent design,
with edible landscapes, ecological building,
and the fundamental desire to work with
Nature, and not against her.

I have been spending a week walking with Tim in what is fondly termed the South Island (the Isle of Wight). This little jewel, which glistens between the Solent and the English Channel, is one of England's treasures. Modest in size, it is home to a surprising variety of habitats and microclimates. Standing on a hillside, we found on one side a chalk downland typical of the coastal region which later in spring and early summer will display a marvellous array of wild flowers and be home to the delicate Adonis Blue butterfly. On the other side of the hill, by contrast, was heathland with its very different flora and fauna. Such variety on just one modest hillside. On the south side of the island, cliff faces and hills are at their highest, dropping rapidly to the sea where sheltered slithers of land provide almost subtropical conditions for gardening. A little further along the coast, walking along its ever-eroding edges and looking down into deep chines (limestone valleys scoured out over millennia by small streams) can prove more dizzying than a roller coaster ride.

As a society, we are obsessed by flying away to exotic locations for our holidays, yet on our own doorsteps is so often a rich variety of resources. The Isle of Wight particularly entrances me because it not only has such variety of habitat, but also still has a great sense of community. When renovating a house there recently, a friend of ours went to order some tiles from a local shop. He asked to leave a deposit and the owner simply told him, "Oh no, sir, we don't do things like that on the island." This trusting attitude is pretty typical – there is a culture of mutual support. Even in the height of the tourist season, people are treated with courtesy and good humour rather than as 'grockles' to be financially exploited. And tucked away in little microclimates are modest gems such as a tiny eleventh century church with medieval frescoes, a place of deep peace. No wonder the Hollywood film director, the late Anthony Minghella, who came from Ryde on the island, fondly paid tribute to this little island whenever he could.

With elements of its community intact and a rich biodiversity, it is no surprise that the Isle of Wight is now becoming a Transition Island. Its energy descent plan is to be entirely self-sufficient in renewable energy by 2020 using wind, wave, tidal, sun and geothermal and to have the smallest carbon footprint in England. I recently heard Dame Ellen MacArthur speak movingly about the Isle of Wight's plans for sustainability. She talked about how she learned to conserve resources like food, power and water which were like gold dust on her record breaking round-the-world yacht races. She went on to say that sailing a boat single-handedly across an ocean forces you to understand sustainability. If you run out of almost any resource you carry, you could die. The island is nearer that state perhaps than the mainland and Peak Oil and climate change will only emphasise this vulnerability. That is why this South Island is less complacent than the North Island.

We seem addicted to escaping to foreign destinations and yet our experience of travel is often one of the tower block culture of industrial tourism with its unsympathetic resource-guzzling developments and despoilment of entire landscapes. I couldn't help smiling at the corporate fiasco of Heathrow's Terminal 5. Before the baggage handling cock up, it was heralded as one of the great post-modernist developments of our 21st century industrial era. It is perhaps more of a whimper, the last flexing of muscles of a dying oil age. Where will this industry be when oil is $200 a barrel?

Before you all sail off to the Isle of Wight in search of its Holy Grail of unspoilt simplicity and warmth, the truth is that if you look carefully you can still find places like it in a place near you. We have an unfortunate cultural habit of undervaluing what is beneath our noses and of being seduced by the exotic. One aspect of a deepening understanding of ecology and culture will be a shift in attitude regarding the familiar. Tim and I have a game in which we see our most common birds, like pigeons and crows, as marvels of the air. We watch the aeronautical grace of the rare pigeagle and crowbuzzard. Imagine if we could train ourselves to see the natural world with all its precious resources afresh, like a round-the-world yachtswoman who has to carefully consider every amp of power used, every meal and drop of water consumed. Far from becoming shrunken and parsimonious, we would conserve every sunbeam, savour every morsel and celebrate the fierce effortlessness of Crow and the gliding nonchalance of Pigeon. We would see with new eyes.

# 57 | Autumn 2008

Tim and I recently attended an ethical business awards ceremony in London. We were there to network and meet some truly inspirational people: Fair traders, people who reinvest their money in apprenticeship schemes in producer countries, dedicated organic farmers, social and ecoproduct innovators, conservationists … Amidst the genuine and the worthy, however, was the inevitable commercialisation of 'Green' with its drive to flog yet more stuff – albeit eco-stuff – for the sake of the Bottom Line. Business as usual then, just eco-style. There was also the claim that the ethical/green sector had 'arrived'. We are now 'glamorous' and 'glitzy' we were told, as if this is a good thing. I spoke to a green marketing guru who, within a minute of learning who I was, zealously told me that *PM* needed to 'rebrand' itself. I think she meant a new title, more glossy paper and pages of advertising and trivia about stuff. I didn't wait to ask. We came away early feeling rather dispirited, paralysingly unable/unwilling to talk-the-talk and, perhaps appropriate for ecobuild enthusiasts, like we were 'round pegs in a square hole'. We both just wanted to go home.

Travelling back on the train we talked about our sense of kinship and belonging with the unglamorous and unglitzy; with the gardeners, woodspeople, ecobuilders and activists who aren't in it for the money, but are in it for their passionate love of our planet. We also agreed that we are fortunate to work with many people of inspiration and integrity. It is a privilege and a joy, for instance, to be in the final stages of producing Ben Law's forthcoming book, *The Woodland Year*, because he so genuinely lives what he writes.

Having grumbled about award ceremonies, I want to tell you why we applied for, and won, the Queen's Award for Enterprise in the Sustainable Development category, deemed the most prestigious award for business in the UK. For nearly two decades we have been conducting our work on the 'edge', as alternative publishers, and usually swimming against the mainstream. At times we relish our difference, our round peg syndrome, but much of the time we have had to live on our wits, flying by the seat of our pants, and it has been a struggle financially and sometimes psychologically.

Joanna Macy, the deep ecologist, often speaks of a centuries-old Tibetan prophecy. It foretells of a time when the forces of destruction are so strong that 'barbarian powers' can destroy not only themselves but the whole world. In this era, the prophecy tells of the arising of Shambhala warriors who, with the heat of compassion and the power of cool insight, are able to dismantle the very citadels of power that threaten humanity's survival, from the inside. "Made by the human mind, they can be unmade by the human mind. The Shambhala warriors know that the dangers threatening life on Earth are not visited on us by any extraterrestrial power, satanic deities, or pre-ordained evil fate. They arise from our own decisions, our own lifestyles, and our own relationships." I make no claims of warriorship, but I do believe in the concept of dismantling thought forms and of introducing new ones. If our differences arise from how we think, rather than from qualities like malice or greed, then it follows that as we dismantle these unhelpful, destructive perspectives, we begin a process whereby new perspectives can be entertained and adopted. This removes the concept of division, of 'them' and 'us', and begins a movement towards a culture of greater tolerance, co-operation and sustainable perspectives.

Returning to the Queen's Award, it seemed time to try to take our message into the heart of the mainstream and into the citadels of Whitehall, to be proud of what we do and who we represent. It did however come as quite a surprise that we actually won it! Rather than being patronised or met by suspicion, we were celebrated with respect and interest. It is natural to question whether 'green' is being 'assimilated' and therefore disarmed by the forces of unsustainability – and I think it is when making money is the primary motive – but I meet many people, some influential, who have woken up to our human predicament and who genuinely care about the fate of all humanity, not just the privileged denizens of the global industrialised North. This is where we are prepared to be counted – open to all people, encouraging big shifts in perspectives in our collective decisions, our lifestyles and our relationships – and where, with the support of all your collective will, we will continue to stand.

In *PM46*, Rob Hopkins wrote an article 'Prepare For Life Without Oil') about 10 things we can do to prepare for a post-carbon future. Number three on his list was 'Get Out of Debt'. He predicted that once oil prices rose there would be sticky financial times ahead and it wouldn't be good to owe money. He recommended eliminating as much of our credit as possible and making getting out of debt a family priority, even if it meant selling the house and living in a smaller one. He even suggested we halve our incomes and make more time for developing skills, useful for the post-oil future, like growing food and ecobuilding. Prophetic words from the master of Transition Culture.* I'd like to make another prediction here. Our current practice in industrialised nations is to split families up and live separately. College/university students move away from home at great expense to themselves (student loans) or their parents when similar courses are often available on their doorstep; working adults often live in houses with rooms to spare; and the elderly either live alone and struggle to cope or, when they become too frail, go into expensive care homes. We are programmed to inhabit our 'castles', whatever the cost, but sharing space and resources are things we will have to relearn how to do.

How we look after our elderly people speaks volumes about our society and its social sustainability. I remember watching a film by Helena Norberg-Hodge, 'Paradise With Side Effects', about two Ladakhi women on a trip to England that was part of an International Society For Ecology & Culture (ISEC) 'reality tour' for community leaders. The tours introduce Ladakhi people to everyday life in the West as it really is, thereby helping to balance some of the glamorised images of the modern world. In one episode, Helena took the Ladakhis to an old people's home. It was with unbearable poignancy that they met an elderly woman who sat for hours in her room in front of a television, obviously terribly lonely. The women were moved to tears and asked, "Where are her family? Where are her children?" It was inconceivable to them to have all the wealth of the West but no family, no stimulation or a sense of community.

In a society that is fragmented, we ghetto-ise our age groups. Increasingly, we see the tendency towards the young roaming in gangs, our elderly living alone in medical facilities, and the interconnection between generations fragmenting. When this happens, tolerance, compassion and respect between generations are lost, and we criticise and prey upon each other. With this on my mind, I sent out a call for material to the Global Ecovillage Network, asking how they take care of their elders. I knew that some ecovillages have youth houses where teenagers can live together and test the boundaries of growing up whilst remaining within the protection and guidance of the wider community.

* www.transitionnetwork.org

But what do ecovillagers plan to do with the 1960s baby boomer generation as they grow older? Capra Carruba heard my call and submitted 'The Golden Age', an article all about how Damanhur in Italy cares for its elderly and crucially, what the elderly are able to offer their community. I learned from Capra – and from my own recent experience caring for my elderly mother – that when we are able to create the right environment, old age can be gilded. The final age of life is not one of action or crushing inaction, but one of belonging and learning simply how to 'be'. In our fast and fragmented world, it is important that one generation at least holds the Zen-like capacity of gentle observation and stillness.

I am also reminded of Joanna Macy's perspective about the melt-down of the industrial growth society and the destruction of our global environment. Joanna, champion of the The Great Turning movement,* questions whether we are in death-bed attendance to a dying age or midwives to a new civilisation. She suggests that we need to be able to hold an unwavering gaze in the face of uncertainty. We do not know what is in store for us, economically or ecologically. What seems obvious though is that we are holding not only our human survival in the balance, but also the survival of many other species. If we can summon the courage to unflinchingly face our predicament, we will not succumb to denial or inaction. Instead, we will have the capacity to raise ourselves up into the power of our convictions and affect positive, life-enhancing changes in our own lives, in the lives of those around us and in our wider society. This is the time to be brave.

*   www.joannamacy.net

After the Crash…

Permaculture is primarily a thinking tool for designing low carbon, highly productive systems; houses, gardens, farms, communities, even businesses … It has a set of principles that ground the theory in practical applications. They are disarmingly simple at first viewing but have a wisdom that deepens as we apply them. During the economic crisis in which the behemoth that is the world's financial system has begun to disintegrate, I have returned to those principles again and again. One is particularly pertinent: 'Use small and slow solutions – The bigger they are, the harder they fall'. Our industrial society depends on vast inputs of fossil fuels whilst our biosphere is poisoned by their outputs. Currently, we have a three day 'just in time' supply chain of supermarkets and we fly, ship and truck stuff in from all over the world. If the fuel supply is interrupted, the supermarket shelves will empty at an alarming rate and panic buying will ensue. Looking to the future, we need to build resilience into our systems by relocalising our essential needs as much as possible and having technological alternatives that we can fix. The more accessible and fixable our technology and the more local our chains of supply are, the more robust the system. This applies to energy, transport, water and housing as well as food.

Near the end of last year, Tim and I spent a blissful week walking in Cornwall. We stayed on a farm in a small but comfortable converted pigsty and explored the empty coves and bustling harbours nearby. We set ourselves the challenge to eat as locally as possible and it was easy. We could buy local fruit and veg, local award winning cheeses and cider and country wines from farm shops. The butcher in the village had a thriving business selling local farmers' livestock and we could eat fish off the quay freshly caught that morning. Despite the presence of the main supermarkets in the big towns, Cornwall is managing to preserve some of its smallholdings, farms and local food links and the tourist industry has provided a seasonal market which encourages some positive aspects of local distinctiveness. The food certainly tasted great and we enjoyed talking to the growers by roadside stalls, the fishmongers on the quay and the farm shop retailer who knew his Cornish cheeses intimately. The local potatoes, grown in loamy earth so red it looked like a pigment, were so delicious we took home a sack for the kids, along with other tasty local treats – fortunately, our girls are foodies and appreciate fine fare.

Back home it isn't so easy. There are less stalls by the roadside selling home produce and the farmers' market is expensive. The fabric that weaves together local food is less coherent. There are too many pony paddocks, not enough smallholdings. Our advantage lies in our garden and we are busy planning how we can increase the range of food we grow throughout the year and how to preserve and store it. I realise that we are lucky to have the garden and that many do not. I am therefore always interested in stories that encourage us all to become more self-reliant. I like stories about how two people turned some overgrown allotments into a thriving community resource; how the humble nettle is more than a weed; it's a spring green, a beer, a soup; how to grow food all year round or organic apples in tiny spaces; even build a den or dwelling with your friends for virtually nothing … As the world's financial system unravels and the dogs of war bay more loudly for resources, the task for us all in 2009 is to focus on how we can become more self-reliant and more resilient as individuals, families and communities. Then we need to share this information with whoever will use it.

I am always fascinated to read about the madness of globalised trading so when reader Val Grainger, aka The Woolly Shepherd, contacted me about the comings and goings of deer in the UK, I pricked up my ears. Woodland coppice is gradually being brought back into rotation here in Britain, but one problem is that deer love to eat the young shoots of coppice regrowth thus killing the stools. Over 150,000 deer are consequently culled in Britain each year and this figure needs to rise to protect the woodlands (we just can't fence it all). Most of this venison is exported to Europe whilst we in Britain import venison from New Zealand in vast quantities to be processed and packaged and sold as British venison. Val says, "This is freely available unadulterated, woodland meat. I have eight acres of woodland on the smallholding and we have lots of deer that do terrible damage. If forest gardening is to be encouraged, this wonderful resource should be harvested and not exported!"

Someone who has done much to raise awareness of forest gardening and permaculture this year is the filmmaker Rebecca Hosking, who made the BBC2 film 'A Farm For The Future' with her partner, Tim Green, exploring Peak Oil and potential answers for oil-free farming. Millions of viewers have watched it and the ripple effect is still evident. (If you missed it, see www.permaculture.co.uk/videos for the online version.) Rebecca told me that it took more than two years of negotiation to persuade the BBC to commission a film about Peak Oil and alternatives to oil-dependent farming (they didn't want to alarm people), yet oil geologists reliably inform us that the world's supply of oil peaked in 2008 at the latest. The world of energy descent is upon us. Overcoming mainstream inertia can be trying.

In the film 'Garbage Warrior', Michael Reynolds, the originator of Earthships (passive solar buildings built using recycled materials and renewable technology), tells the story of how the New Mexico state banned him from building experimental structures. He speaks colourfully of his struggle to overturn legislation, "I am not trying to bad-mouth the system. I have become a Trojan horse. I have infiltrated the system. I have crawled up the asshole and I am going to change them from the bloodstream." He succeeded ... *PM*, in print since 1992, spent its early life outside the system, trying to engage the mainstream. Now we are invited to share our views at the London International Book Fair and with the Queen's Award for Enterprise panel – bastions of capitalism. Are we in danger of losing our radical edge and forgetting where we came from? I don't think so. We are consciously trying to use the system to spread our ideas as far as possible. We understand that time is very short in terms of climate change and strategies for adaptation are vital now. In the short term, we can't reverse the clock. Global temperature rises during this century are unavoidable. The significant question is what can we do for our grandchildren?

I am interested in how people respond to climate change and Peak Oil. Is it with denial, fear and depression or with enquiry and subsequent positive actions? The film critic, Dr Emily D Edwards, writes about what purpose films like 'The Last Stand' (an environmental documentary) serve: "For the dissident audience, the mission is to corrode the mantra of development equals progress, jobs and a strong economy. For an apathetic audience, the mission is to open a wedge in the indifference. For younger audiences, the mission is to educate and recruit a new generation to activism. For sympathetic audiences, the mission is to inspire and energize the troops." *PM* aims to be a window on a world of alternatives to the fossil fuel dominated, centralised power, global markets model – what David Holmgren calls 'Brown Tech'. We want to open a wedge in the indifference with our collective passion for positive change, celebrate the power of reclaiming self-reliance in a world of crumbling financial systems, and show people that there are other, better ways of living. Activist Joanna Macy recommends we close our eyes and remember three non-consumer things we are pleased about that have occurred in the last 24 hours, "Self appreciation in a culture that's trying to sell us things is deeply subversive."

Tim and I recently visited Devon to see the Hoskings' farm which was featured in BBC2's 'A Farm For The Future'. The farm dramatically contrasts the neighbouring barren, over-ploughed agricultural desert drenched in fertilisers. On her farm there are huge ancient hedgerows full of nesting birds and old standard apple trees, pastures that haven't been ploughed for 500 years full of orchids, buzzing with life, nesting birds, and a stream meandering though muddy flats full of yellow flag irises. Quite honestly, I haven't seen a farm like this since I was a very little girl visiting Connemara in Ireland in the sixties. Every summer, my family used to stay on a mixed farm by the shore of Loch Corrib. The land teemed with biodiversity and the loch was full of wild brown trout, perch and monstrously large pike. Rebecca Hosking asked me how I saw permaculture developing on the farm. She also told me how many of the neighbours thought the family were crazy for farming this way, without huge inputs of NPK (agricultural 'whizz' she calls it), encouraging foxes on to the land to keep the rabbit population in balance and quietly encouraging as much fauna and flora on to the farm as possible. I hope the time is coming when they will be appreciated as genuine pioneers. I didn't tell her how to run her farm though I did encourage the family to open it to the public so that they can take a tour and appreciate the intelligent dedication and vision of her father who refused to farm 'conventionally'.

After the Hoskings' farm we visited Martin Crawford at the Agroforestry

Research Trust. My cup of happiness overflowed as I walked his two acres of forest garden. At times, it was like walking through a subtropical jungle full of edible, medicinal and useful plants. I was struck by the beauty of trees like the Chinese dogwood and the majestic grace of the Rhubarb Australe. Tim and I came away empowered. We planted a forest garden/ wildlife garden in the early nineties, but raising children and publishing have rather got in the way of its development. We realised we hadn't done a bad job, however, and had developed similar techniques to Martin. Hard work this year has brought the whole garden on enormously and planting more ground cover and some additional trees and shrubs in our forest garden this autumn will almost complete the design. Martin deeply inspired us.

My other preoccupation this year – as my long-suffering family will agree – has been growing food under glass. It's easy to grow fruit and veg in summer and autumn, but how are we to feed ourselves all winter and spring if we are truly planning a transition away from imported food? I set about entirely renovating our storm damaged greenhouse and making cold frames. I have learnt that before we had fossil fuels to heat greenhouses, the Dutch were experts in growing under glass. Introducing a cold frame over the greenhouse border allows all year growing. This autumn I'll be planting oriental stir fry vegetables like tatsoi, mibuna and mizuna, and plants like hardy cornsalad and winter carrots (other suggestions welcome). My research has made me ponder on just how much knowledge previous generations had. We will have no choice but to undertake a journey of rediscovery and rekindle our lost skills. It will be like exploring a collective unconscious that we currently only vaguely acknowledge, but which is vast and powerful. The future is waiting for us and I refuse to imagine that it is tormented and dark.

I have been pondering the United Nations Climate Change Conference taking place this December in Copenhagen. Government leaders will gather from all over the world in an attempt to agree a plan to reduce $CO_2$ in the atmosphere. They will argue about how we can do this whilst maintaining economic growth. They may even talk about biofuels, aviation and new technologies that could make it all possible. They'll reach an agreement that will keep industry growing and make token attempts at reducing carbon to justify it. At the end of the event, they will sign a big document, make fine speeches and go home. That's my prediction. I hope I am wrong. Surely if the effects are so serious our leaders should be doing everything possible to make this conference count and create effective international policies? Unfortunately, they are reactive, not proactive. They are sponsored by powerful lobbies who have vested interests in maintaining industrial growth. Politicians are the tails, not the dogs.

One of the problems with climate change is that it is hard to appreciate how desperate the situation really is and the science is also difficult to understand – it involves vast interrelated planetary systems, feedback mechanisms and timescales.

There is an interesting approach to simplifying ways of talking about atmospheric $CO_2$. It is called the 350 Movement (www.350.org). Since the start of the industrial age, the amount of $CO_2$ in the atmosphere has increased by 42%, from 280 parts per million (ppm) to 387ppm.

350ppm is what scientists say is the 'safe' upper limit for $CO_2$ in the atmosphere. As we continue to burn coal, oil and gas, $CO_2$ is increasing every year by 2ppm. We are heading for 450ppm. The level needs to be 350. The 350 Movement is mobilising people and holding events, with members from over 131 countries. I urge you to join in. As Martin Luther King said, "Our lives begin to end the day we become silent about things that matter."

Another of the problems is that a significant number of people think climate change is now unstoppable – that we will not return to 350ppm in time. The growth machine – unrestrained capitalism, 'development', human folly, call it what you will – has become such a relentless force that it will spell the end of human civilisation. Feedback systems are kicking in. A simple example of this is the shrinking polar ice caps. Ice is white and reflects sunlight/heat into outer space. As the temperature increases and the ice melts, the ice caps become smaller and the oceans become bigger. The water absorbs heat, and thus makes it warmer which in turn melts more ice, reflecting back less heat. Other people believe that though climate change has hit runaway levels which far exceed the conservative estimate of the Intergovernmental Panel on Climate Change (IPCC), it can still be mitigated. We'll have to adapt in the short term but there is a chance we won't heat our planet to the point when we fry ourselves out of existence. I have no doubt however that many people are thinking and acting ... People want to find positive ways of living more low carbon lifestyles. There is an ongoing shift in society, but it is still relatively small.

Where do I sit in all this? I have to admit I don't know. I read, try to unravel the complexities, and sway between unstoppable (bad day) and runaway (good day). In many ways, it makes no difference to my actions. Joanna Macy speaks of the capacity to 'sustain the gaze'. We are here to witness an unprecedented change in human history. We must not become passive or flinch into denial at this critical moment. Yet whilst there is even a tiny opportunity to turn down the heat for future generations, I want to be part of that movement. I don't want to 'become silent about things that matter'. Nor do I want to change how I live, growing food, helping establish an educational centre, working on wider life-enhancing projects like Gaia Education, learning to love … These are good things to do. And if it is too late? Well, I doubt I'd go on a transglobal aviation binge. I'd carry on exploring the good ways of living that are so eloquently and creatively expressed in these pages and work on sustaining the gaze. And after all … nothing is certain.

" There is a pleasure in the pathless woods,
There is a rapture on the lonely shore,
There is society, where none intrudes,
By the deep Sea, and music in its roar:
I love not Man the less, but Nature more,
From these our interviews, in which I steal
From all I may be, or have been before,
To mingle with the Universe, and feel
What I can ne'er express, yet cannot all conceal.

**George Gordon Byron**
*Childe Harold's Pilgrimage*

# Section Four

# 2010 - 2013

World population is 6.84 billion.

**12 January 2010**, 7.0 magnitude earthquake devastates Port-au-Prince, Haiti. It is the region's worst earthquake in 200 years. Permaculturists provide strategic skills and aid.

**14 April 2010**, an explosion in the Eyjafjallajökull volcano in Iceland results in a volcanic ash plume in the atmosphere over northern and central Europe.

**20 April 2010**, an explosion on a BP oil drilling rig off the coast of Louisiana kills 11 people and injures 17. Experts estimate 42,000 gallons of crude oil per hour spills into the Gulf of Mexico. It is finally capped on 15 July.

**13 June 2010**, the United States finds more than $1 trillion in mineral resources in the mountains of Afghanistan which include previously unknown deposits of iron, copper, gold, and lithium. Now we know why the country is so strategic to the West.

**13 October 2010**, 33 trapped Chilean miners are rescued after spending 68 days trapped in a mine half a mile underground.

**21 November 2010**, the Irish government requests a $100 billion bailout package from the European Union and IMF to help save its flailing economy.

**11 January 2011**, the Arab Spring movement begins in Tunisia when demonstrators take to the streets to protest chronic unemployment and police brutality.

**2 May 2011**, US troops and CIA operatives shoot and kill Osama bin Laden in Abbottabad, Pakistan.

**17 October 2011**, Occupy Wall Street, an organised protest in New York's financial district, expands to other cities across the USA.

**28 November to 11 December 2011**, United Nations Climate Change Conference (COP17) is held in Durban, South Africa. Scientists warn that the deal discussed is not sufficient to avoid global warming beyond 2°C.

**4 March 2012**, Vladimir Putin wins the presidential election in Russia, claiming 64% of the vote. It will be his third full term as president of Russia.

**12 February 2013**, North Korea says it has detonated a third nuclear bomb.

**13 March 2013**, Cardinal Jorge Mario Bergoglio of Argentina is elected as the new Pope Francis, succeeding Benedict XVI.

**9 June 2013**, Edward Snowden, a former CIA employee, admits that he is the source of leaks about the top-secret surveillance activities of the National Security Agency.

In the permaculture world, Ben Law builds a round wood timber frame woodland hall at The Sustainability Centre, near our office, in 2010. At the same time we produce his book, *Roundwood Timber Framing: Building Naturally Using Local Resources*. Art imitates life.

In 2011, Permanent Publications publishes *Designing Ecological Habitats: Creating a Sense of Place* edited by E. Christopher Mare and Max O. Lindegger, respected permaculture teacher and designer from Crystal Waters, Australia. This is the third volume in the Gaia Education Four Keys to Sustainability series. Mark Richards from UNESCO writes the foreword.

The next year Permanent Publications publishes *Permaculture Design – Step by Step* by Aranya, a Permaculture Design Course in a nutshell, later translated into multiple languages. Also published are *People & Permaculture* by Looby Macnamara, the first ever book exploring the use of permaculture design for peoplecare, and *The Moneyless Manifesto: Live Well, Live Rich, Live Free* by Mark Boyle, a follow-up to his bestseller, *The Moneyless Man*. It is full of zero cost permaculture thinking. The book is also available free online – an experiment in gift economy thinking. Will we sell enough books to pay the print bill? We did. But only just. The Gift Economy works but only if the relationship is two ways. Luckily, enough people got that and were prepared to invest in the print edition of the book.

In the Harland world, our daughters have now grown into beautiful young women. Hayley is developing her singer/songwriting and production skills. Then she embarks on a journey of self-discovery that includes studying healing, yoga, taking a Permaculture Design Course and learning about regenerative agriculture with Darren Doherty. Gail completes college and decides not to go to university. Instead she fills a backpack almost as big as her small frame and goes to Malawi for six months. There she too studies permaculture and volunteers on various projects. She returns home to live and to study holistic massage in Brighton. I am excited to see them both growing up and finding their own paths, whilst both learning skills and knowledge in areas that are dear to us.

With the kids having left home, Tim and I do not have an empty nest, however. My mother's dementia is progressive and so she comes to live at the end of our road in sheltered housing. By 2010-13 she is becoming very frail. I discover, at first hand, the gaping holes in the NHS system. Despite her severe medical problems, I cannot get a district nurse to visit her and advise me on incontinence and the realities of dementia as they are so understaffed. Nor will my GP make house calls to her when she is ill. At first, Social Services assess her and refuse all provision of care. Then when they re-assess her, they appoint a local care company who constantly switch around their underpaid staff between clients and misbill me for visits my mother has not received. My mother's confusion and distress deepens and I withdraw her from care managed by Social Services and I organise my own network of professional help. Tim and I feel very alone and abandoned by the system, struggling to understand and cope with dementia, and the day-to-day demands of looking after an elderly person with severe short-term memory loss. That said, my mother is infallibly cheerful and appreciative of the love and support she receives. Her spirit is strong and her gratitude is deeply touching. She wants to stay at home, not be put into a home. We do all we can to make her life easier. The *PM* team are very understanding and cover me when I have to respond to a domestic crisis. Tim is my rock. Without him I couldn't possibly be a primary carer, run a publishing company, or be Chair of the Board of Trustees at The Sustainability Centre.

*The most important change that people can make is to change their way of looking at the world. We can change studies, jobs, neighbourhoods, even countries and continents and still remain much as we always were. But change our fundamental angle of vision and everything changes – our priorities, our values, our judgements, our pursuits. Again and again ... this total upheaval in the imagination has marked the beginning of a new life ... a turning of the heart, a 'metanoia', by which [human beings] see with new eyes and understand with new minds and turn their energies to new ways of living.*

BARBARA WARD
Writer and economist, in a paper on global governance: www.gdrc.org/u-gov/global-neighbourhood/chap2.htm

*Permaculture* magazine is all about – an openness to explore new ideas and place them in context with what we have found to be already useful ... We want to understand what kind of technologies and buildings will work best, well before oil and gas become scarce; how we will grow our food without easy access to fossil fuels for fertilisers and transport; and how we can shape our communities constructively to face these challenges. Vitally, we need to become more economically resilient and 'find our power' (Chris Johnstone's words) to redesign the building blocks of a sustainable human culture. These will enable us not only to endure and thrive, but allow other species to do so as well. These are big questions that we have touched on in our 20 years of publishing, and they are uppermost in our minds.

This is the time when we need to see the world with new eyes and feel the call for a fresh adventure. There is, however, a dangerous resistance to change. Recent news reports have focused on the Intergovernmental Panel on Climate Change (IPCC) and the Climatic Research Unit (CRU) in Norwich exaggerating or 'simplifying' their data. The IPCC report claimed that Himalayan glaciers would melt in 25 years but got it wrong by a factor of 10 – they are expected to disappear within 250 years. Not helpful in the battle to counter scepticism, but given that most of northern India and almost all of Pakistan depend on the glacial water for their agriculture, this is still devastating news. The UK House of Commons Science and Technology Committee and an independent scientific panel have now dismissed these smears of 'bad science'. It is no coincidence that these stories first broke around the time of the UN Copenhagen Climate Change Conference in 2009, when the world's nations were trying to seek a deal on global emissions.

Climate change has become such a hot political topic that in 2009, the Center for Public Integrity reported a huge expansion in lobbying by polluting energy interests, leading to over 1,150 groups buying influence as the US Congress sought to pass the Waxman-Markey climate bill. The actual dollar amount spent is unknown, as disclosure laws require few details, but the Center calculated that an extremely conservative estimate would give a minimum figure of more than US$27 million spent in direct lobbying from April to June 2009 alone.

This information begins to quantify the depth of resistance to new ideas. Yet there are also many people around the world who welcome a total 'upheaval of the imagination' and want to explore creative, life-enhancing, problem-solving strategies, designs and solutions. This new adventure will not be easy, but it is vital that we embrace the challenges it will offer and take heart from each other.

# 65 | Autumn 2010

It has been an interesting and creative few months since our last issue. We have been working on three forthcoming books, a film project and a magazine issue. One new book, *Roundwood Timber Framing* by Ben Law, plus a film on the subject, has been unfolding not only on paper and digitally, but in tangible 'woody' reality. Art has literally been imitating life. In a clearing in our woodland at The Sustainability Centre just beyond my window, Ben and his accomplished roundwood framers plus apprentices have been building a woodland classroom. It has been wonderful to watch it arise out of the woods and be a small part of the experience. Much of the timber has been sourced from our overstood plantations here. Years ago when the Centre was in its infancy, foresters working for the County Council came to assess the woodland, left unmanaged for over 50 years and damaged by grey squirrel and deer. They told us the best thing we could do commercially was to clear fell the whole lot and replant. Today Ben and his crew have built us a beautiful building from this maligned timber. He tells me there is still enough suitable timber left for at least four more large buildings.

The classroom's frame and its steam bent roof rafters are made from Lawson cypress, a softwood that is usually pulped for paper or chipped for biomass boilers. Ben has never built with this timber before, but it is abundant here and he uses whatever is available on site whenever possible, and he says the wood is a pleasure to work with. Each frame is individually constructed by hand in the woods and is moved into position for the frame raising. We publishers would down computers and happily participate in lifting the great frames into place. They sit on padstones, each carefully sited, and after raising they are anchored to the earth, literally. The floor joists are Douglas fir and roof shingles are western red cedar, another abundant fast growing wood that can be substituted for oak. The cedar comes from the Cowdray Estate, just over the border in Sussex, more famous for its polo, but also a useful silvicultural resource.

The build itself – sited at the former HMS *Mercury*, an ex-Royal Navy base that is better known for its bomb-proof, rather brutal 1960s buildings – is a beautiful landmark for us. It is a celebration space as well as classroom with a magnificent shingle roof that curves over the building like the hull of a great ship. The northern end holds a Rumford fireplace surrounded by rammed earth cordwood walls and bench, plus an earthen floor sealed with linseed oil. The rest of the floor is boarded western red cedar. The walls are open to the elements (a design that allows for more lenient planning permission and building regulations) and the southern end opens up into a large verandah, soaring out into the woodland. We have been working with Ben as publishers since the 1990s. Now we have an entirely natural building hewn by hand from our own environs, demonstrating what we have believed in and supported for years.

I have been deeply touched whilst researching the article for this issue on Haiti following the earthquake. Reading about the brave and selfless work of people like Rodrigo Silva and Hunter Heaivilin, who have been volunteering there, has been inspirational. They and others from all over the world have been using their specialist skills to make a real difference in this extreme crisis. They have built composting toilets for thousands of people in camps, taught simple methods for making sand and cloth filters to clean water, taught people how to avoid cholera (not easy in a country with a horrific lack of sanitation) and how to identify plants with saponins to maintain better hygiene. There are also people training Haitians in permaculture and reafforestation ('training the trainers') to rebuild food security whilst also encouraging traditional Haitian agriculture.

Haiti has a wonderful growing climate and the potential to produce many types of food in forest gardening systems. It used to be the 'bread basket' of Central America, just as Afghanistan used to be the orchard of the Middle East and a net exporter of quality dried fruit like apricots, raisins and sultanas. Now the people of both countries suffer from malnutrition and are forced to rely on aid. With strategic help and intelligent training, this can be reversed in Haiti (and I hope ultimately in Afghanistan too if global politics allows). Permaculturists are at the cutting edge of this work, providing replicable, low cost solutions and building networks to pass on this information, often working for expenses and food only. The conditions they work in are often unimaginably grim. Let's celebrate and support them.

Back home in the 'one-third world', we enter 2011 suffering few of the problems that beset the so-called 'third world'. Nonetheless recession is biting. People have a lot less money, many have lost their jobs, and swingeing cuts have affected charities and NGOs. Social and commercial enterprises are being squeezed and are failing. Few of us are immune. This is unpleasant and frightening but it has its positive face as well. As times get tougher, many people are looking for ways of adapting creatively to a changing world. Inevitably, there will be an exploration of ideas and practical strategies that will help us through times of instability and difficult transition. We will need to reskill in new technologies, ideas and practices to adapt. (Paul Allen explains the Centre for Alternative Technology's contribution in this issue.) Increasingly, many of us are learning how to grow food, save money, preserve our resources, live more intelligently and simply, and design our own careers in ways that our parents and grandparents could not have imagined possible.

The key to successful adaptation is not necessarily based on acquisition (ideas, practices, 'stuff') but on our dedication to living creatively. I believe the secret is to find our joy and not to feel this is gloomy work that 'must' be done. Enjoying simplicity and creating a sense of community is a very powerful response to consumerism. It frees us from judging ourselves in relation to what we own and reduces our dependence on money. It takes us beyond a culture of competition and division. Living this way should not be 'holier than thou' – professing to have all the answers – or a painful moral obligation. It is an exploration of new territories of the mind and heart. For me, the essence of permaculture is creative, positive, problem-solving, generous with skills and time, and fun too.

I awake in the deep velvety dark of the night to write. Everything is changing. My psyche feels an unravelling, a flexing of the new. It was predicted years ago, not always in apocalyptic terms because change opens to the possibilities of undreamt opportunity. I won't catalogue the recent societal and global changes – I am sure you know – but I sense that we humans are becoming ever more aware of how interconnected we really are, to both the human and planetary systems. As we force the envelope of our current modus operandi on this Earth, we are experiencing greater and greater feedback. This makes us feel vulnerable, as though we are part of an endgame we do not control. There is another narrative, however, that does not deny the reality of unfolding world events, yet it does challenge the assumption that we are powerless to effect positive change.

I recently visited a project that opened my eyes to how radically effective Earth restoration projects can be. This was not a big UN or intergovernmental programme, but one run by a small ecovillage community with the help of a relentlessly confident and visionary man, Sepp Holzer. I had heard he was building lakes in the arid Iberian Peninsula in Portugal. I imagined that they would be reasonably impressive after the winter rains. I had even watched a webcam of the first lake filling up last year. I had no concept of the scale of the restoration work, however. Sepp and the Tamera community* have literally dammed a valley and stopped

the rain and topsoil rushing down the valley and into the sea.

Ever decreasing yields in this depopulated, rural region have driven poor farmers to try and extract more from the land than it is capable of bearing. Sheep are stocked at such density that the pasture is destroyed. Nature responds to the overgrazing by growing a 'scab', the inedible rock rose, *Cistus* spp., often the first pioneer after wildfire. 90% of the remnant cork oak forests are dying due to soil compaction that destroys soil mycorrhiza. The rest are being felled as cork falls out of favour, replaced by eucalyptus, hungry exotics in a brittle landscape. With the oaks dies a unique, biodiverse habitat and the Iberian lynx and Bonelli's eagle are threatened with extinction.

Sepp and the Tamerans have reversed this process in their valley. They stopped the overgrazing and ploughing, focusing the community's food production on fruit and vegetables. There are raised beds every-where full of annual and perennial veg. Fruit and nut trees line the banks of the lakes. The winterbourne stream is dammed and there is an interconnected system of lakes that flow into each other as the slope falls down the valley. It is almost unbeliev-able that in such an arid landscape, so much water can be collected. This is living water too, with rippling surfaces, filled with frogs and fish, to keep the balance between mosquitoes and humans healthy. Sepp cups his hands and tells us, "God gives us

* www.tamera.org

enough water. All we have to do is find a way of holding it in the landscape."

What has been achieved in just three years is astonishing. Early morning mists arise out of the lakes and leave their dew on the surrounding plants. Swallows swoop and drink. Otters have returned. New springs rise in the surrounding slopes. The younger oaks are seeding and growing. Even a Bonelli's eagle has visited. Perhaps it will return this year with a mate. The whole landscape is being reaquified. My heart opens in the knowledge that we can restore the Earth. This story must be a part of our new narrative.

I have been slowly reading a book for the last few months, a few pages at a time, like savouring a good meal. It is *The Biochar Solution* by Albert Bates. I met Albert at the Ecovillage Conference at Findhorn in 1995. He was an established permaculture teacher and leading light of the ecovillage movement and I was an unknown editor. It was an amazing event where the Global Ecovillage Network was founded.

Albert interested me. A former environmental rights lawyer, paramedic, brick mason, horse trainer, he is proud to be a permaculturist, ecovillage designer and natural builder – he is a polymath. You might think this book might be dry and factual but you would be wrong. Albert is a storyteller. He describes an epic adventure through pre-Conquistador South America where the black soils of the indigenous people, 'terra preta' made from biochar mixed with kitchen compost, were so fertile they supported sophisticated cultures in cities deep in the Amazon. The Europeans invaded these lands, fought the inhabitants and imported infectious diseases and viruses that decimated the indigenous population. As Amazonian civilisations died out, the forest reclaimed the land.

"So great was the burst of vegetation over open fields and mounded cities that the carbon drawn from the air to feed this greening upset atmospheric chemistry. Analysis of the soils and lake sediment of both pre-contact population centers and sparsely populated surrounding regions reveals that the reforestation of land following the collapse drew so much carbon out of the atmosphere so rapidly that Europe literally froze."* My childhood history lessons – stories of the Thames freezing over and of Europe being so cold that Louis XIV installed parquet floors in the Palace of Versailles – have been entirely reframed.

When these civilisations died out, with them were lost agricultural sciences developed over millennia and the recipe of terra preta. There follows a journey through the history of agriculture: the rise and fall of civilisations who exhausted their soils; an exploration of self-sustaining and highly sophisticated indigenous organic polycultures (oh, how arrogant we are in the West thinking we are 'civilised' with our chemical, oil-based monocultures!); carbon farming techniques; the production of biochar that makes soils capable of supporting huge colonies of micro-organisms, creating symbiosis between soil and plants; and how to lock up carbon in the soil. There is also a calculated rationale on how many people are needed to grow, plant and care for enough trees to reforest the planet. All these techniques will stabilise the global climate – indeed cool it – and within a few decades if we act in concord and quickly. This is permaculture design applied to global climate change. It is BIG systems thinking broken down into bite size chunks and presented as an interrelated web of practical, scientifically researched solutions.

---

* *The Biochar Solution*, Albert Bates, New Society Publishers, 2010, p.35.

I have been meeting remarkable people who are undeterred by the collective inaction of the status quo and are 100% committed to building a new world. Polly Higgins, the barrister who is campaigning for a UN amendment to outlaw the deliberate destruction of ecosystems, is one of them. Like Albert, Polly has fuelled my resolve to carry on doing what I can to effect change.

A recent trip to the Houses of Parliament, London reminded me that positive change is unlikely to stem from the Western establishment or the enriched nations of the Orient, but it could come from the global voice of the 'indigenous' of all nations. This is me and you, my friends. We share a bond beyond race, ethnicity, class, nationality, education, religion … We share a love for the Earth and its people, and our deepest concern for the future. Yes, another world is possible, but only if we believe we can make the change. Choose your strategy, your campaign, your activism, your research, your passion – however humble – and stick to it not for a year or two, but for the rest of your lives. Speak up. Seek the company of like minds, of inspirational people. Treat every day as a miracle. Don't give up and become bitter when things don't go your way. Be here for the long haul.

I recently interviewed barrister, Polly Higgins, who is proposing to the UN that Ecocide, the environmental equivalent of Genocide, becomes the fifth International Crime Against Peace, alongside Genocide, Crimes Against Humanity, Crimes of Aggression and War Crimes. Polly and a group of UK barristers and lawyers are also drafting an Ecocide Act for the Houses of Parliament. What does this mean and why is it relevant to us?

The proposed new law of Ecocide is seen as fundamental to addressing humanitarian and environmental issues on a global scale. Currently, the Earth has no rights in law and Ecocide would protect the Earth's Right to Life. It would outlaw corporate Earthslaughter and close the door on commercial activities that destroy ecosystems. Currently, the world invests billions in technologies based on fossil fuels. Ecocide would sway the balance and stimulate investment in a new generation of clean technologies. It is not about prosecuting CEOs and corporate bodies, but about requiring 'superior responsibility' from companies, changing how we do business on this planet, and influencing intergovernmental policy and action on climate change. Ecocide is a mechanism that shifts civilisations' understanding of what is acceptable.

Ecocide happens everywhere in our world: Arctic drilling, fracking in the UK, the deforestation of the Amazon, major oil spills in the Gulf of Mexico, bauxite mining from the Niyamgiri mountain in India, tar sand extraction in Canada, deep sea mining of the Central and Eastern Manus Basin … Alone and in small groups, we are powerless to stop it, but together and at national and international levels we can begin to change the odds using the power of law. I urge you to support the campaign (www.eradicatingecocide. com) and if you belong to an NGO or are a member of an environmental campaign ask them to get behind it.

At the end of September I attended an unprecedented event. The UK Supreme Court in London became the venue of a mock Ecocide trail. Two barristers, Michael Mansfield QC for the prosecution, and Chris Parker QC for the defence, together with their legal teams, led a case for and against two fictional CEOs of major corporations. Legal arguments were put as to whether Ecocide and the Earth's Right to Life could be applied to the charges against them (a major oil spill in the Gulf and tar sands extraction in Canada). The trial supposed that Ecocide had indeed been adopted by the UN and was heard in front of judge and jury, as well as press and public. It called upon expert witnesses to give evidence. This was not a piece of theatre, though it was compelling to watch, and nor was it pre-scripted. It had a serious purpose: to examine how the crime of Ecocide protects the Earth's Right to Life. It was a fascinating experience to be in the very midst of British legal procedure and watch some brilliant minds apply themselves to the task. The mock trial saw the prosecution succeeding on two out of three counts but it also offered Polly Higgins' legal team further insights as to how they can improve the draft law.

I was deeply affected by the day, held in the heart of the British Establishment, next to Westminster Abbey and Parliament Square. I met many people who dedicate time, energy and resources to work tirelessly for the Earth. The strong leadership and powerful ethics of people like Polly and Michael Mansfield moved me. This was a consciousness raising exercise and it gave me hope.

We often see people in black and white, as good or bad, them and us. What I saw that day was all about us. We were reminded again that Wilberforce campaigned for years to abolish slavery but it was when the CEO of the British East India Company joined the campaign that the Act went through Parliament. Let's not close the door on solutions because they do not comply with our worldview or because we have been made cynical through disappointment. Let's be open to new possibilities. Our current system is breaking down, but this disintegration will open the door to new ways of working in the world and they may well come from unexpected quarters.

Last summer Tim and I did something different. We went walking along part of the Ridgeway, Britain's oldest road, that runs through central southern England, through the wooded hills and valleys of the Chilterns to the north Wessex Downs, rich in wildlife found in chalk grassland habitats, and down into the World Heritage Site of Avebury. The Ridgeway follows an ancient route over the high ground used since prehistoric times by travellers, herdsmen and soldiers. Close by in the wide rolling landscape are many archaeological treasures: Neolithic and Bronze Age barrows, Iron Age forts, examples of ancient strip farming and the figures of white horses cut into the chalk. It is a landscape alive with the past, a feast of prehistory, Albion at its most monumental.

But this was no ordinary hike. We chose to walk and live 'in community', sharing route and food with a small band of people, mainly rough camping together along the way. We had met the organiser, Graham Joyce, some years ago at a Work That Reconnects training with Joanna Macy. In 2008 Graham organised the 'Awakening Albion'* walk across England from Cornwall to East Anglia along the Michael and Mary ley lines to celebrate the land and walk in community. It took seven weeks. Some of the people involved met again for this shorter walk. We were the 'unknowns'.

Arriving by train in Wiltshire in the Vale of the White Horse, where we were to begin our journey, we could only take what we could carry there and that had to include tent, sleeping bag and mat. By necessity, we had to live simply. Each day we walked, sometimes in community, sometimes alone, but always high up in a landscape offering wonderful panoramic perspectives. Graham, an archaeologist by training, taught us the subtle details of prehistoric forms, of barrow and dyke, and to see traces of ancient humanity's agriculture, still evident on the chalky hills.

The group itself was rich with experience: there were artists, musicians, bushcrafters, herbalists, a teacher, a yurtmaker, yoga practitioners, permaculturists, long-distance walkers … The camp evolved its own rhythm as we walked the hills and valleys each day and we learnt to care for each other, everyone generous with the daily tasks. The warmth of this temporary community was intoxicating. No egos jostled for space, each allowing the others to be nurtured and thrive. I know, it sounds idyllic, and for those brief nine days it was … and we all laughed more than we had for years.

The walk culminated in the ancient landscape of Avebury, having walked at least 10 miles a day, sometimes more, in circuitous routes to get there, and camping in eccentric places (with prearranged permission from the landowners). By then we had entered a state of deep landscape immersion, sensitive to the native plants and creatures, alive to the changes of each hill and valley, and with a feeling of

---

* www.awakeningalbion.com

wellbeing that is hard to explain. Walking, or tramping, had become our meditation.

Our bodies sunk into an awareness that was deeply peaceful. Phillip O'Connor, an articulate vagrant, describes this as an "incomparable feeling … as though one were a prayer winding along a road…" He found that during long periods of tramping a deep mental rhythm, 'poetic in effects', began to dominate all his perceptions. "All hard nodules of concepts are softly coaxed into disbursing their cherished contents … One's 'identify-sense' becomes 'diffused into the landscape'…"* Linear time became irrelevant. We felt immersed in deep time, long, slow and luxuriantly smooth. Avebury itself came alive to me as Graham led us through the ancient turning of the seasons symbolically, the wheel of the year our ancestors so revered that they built great monuments to mark and celebrate this circular time and the miracle of birth, life and death.

I learned so many things in that week: to love the downland landscape even more deeply and to understand it through protracted observation; to appreciate the meditative quality of walking and the aliveness it brings to my desk-bound body; to relish the warmth and humour of community, how gentle and generous people can be and how we all yearn for this intimacy in our lives; and to feel a connection to our ancient past. All this with consuming little and without travelling far…

The turning of our culture from destructive overconsumption to living within our limits can seem impossible whilst we are trapped in the hubbub of normal life, yet I saw in those few days how the future could be. It may seem like a romantic idyll, but it gave me an insight that has left me with an inner fire as hot as the rocket stove we cooked on.

---

* *Symbolic Landscape*, Paul Devereux, Gothic Image Publications, 1992, pp.38-39.

# 73 | Autumn 2012

2012 is certainly turning out to be a memorable year. The jet stream has moved again. It usually passes to the west of Britain and Ireland but it has switched direction and is now lying nearer the English Channel, as it did in 2007-09. This means France and Britain are far wetter than usual. In Britain we ended the winter with a drought and have entered the summer with floods. In the US, extremely dry conditions and erratic winds have caused wildfires in Wyoming with 400 foot walls of flame 'never seen before'. There have also been wildfires in Colorado, a heatwave across the eastern seaboard, and the 'super derecho' across the Midwest – a powerful freak wind storm. Cautiously scientists are linking some of these extreme weather incidents with human-induced climate change. Yet others, like Michael F. Wehner, staff scientist at the Lawrence Berkeley National Laboratory, tell us, "By 2100, today's most extreme weather events will seem relatively normal."*

You could be forgiven for feeling pretty blue after Rio+20's lack of tangible agreement on reducing atmospheric $CO_2$ levels, or even curbing them, with only a toothless statement about 'sustainable growth' on offer. I did. So what can people who are worried about the well-being of future generations do?

There are both micro and macro solutions. We do not regard permaculture as ecoDIY or self-help, although that aspect can be part of the picture. We see permaculture as a design system that can be applied on many scales. In this issue, we meet permaculture designers working on farm designs in different climates; perma-culturists in London building garden sheds out of waste wood; we experiment with preserving food without electricity – the world beyond the fridge – in our DIY solar food dryer; we explore an emerging discipline of biological design using permaculture principles to treat waste and clean up polluted waterways; we also discover experiments in Fukuoka-style biointensive horticulture; we travel to South America to taste Incan crops that can be grown in other temperate climates; we learn how to plant small wildflower patches to help support urban bee popula-tions; and we also enhance personal communication skills as well as learn about site surveying.

You may think this is an eclectic mix of subjects. It is, but there is an underlying rationale. What holds all these subjects together is leading edge thinking and applied design to create low carbon systems which are not just sustainable, but preferably regenerative.

We can apply permaculture ethics and principles on any scale, anywhere: from gardens to farms, sewage treatment systems to entire waterways and indeed watersheds. We can even use them to design effective groups and communities. Some people describe permaculture as an ecological design system. Others see it working

---

* www.guardian.co.uk/environment/blog/2012/jul/03/weather-extreme-blame-global-warming

beyond that, the ethics underpinning a philosophy to live by.

We think how you apply permaculture in your life is your business. And let's be clear, permaculture is not the Holy Grail. There are many strategies, tools and techniques to redesign the way in which we live on this planet. For us, permaculture is an important tool that helps us think holistically to see and integrate the wider picture. Beyond the words, what matters most is that people continue to experiment, test, refine and put into practice positive solutions that enable us to restore ecosystems, heal social divides and create more harmonious, low carbon societies. We want to inspire and engage people in this process.

We think it is imperative that we build a global movement able to overcome its differences and work out effective processes that force serious attention on climate change and the consequences of ecosystem destruction. We need to stop disembowelling each other about which pathway is best. We need to start thinking strategically, work together with synthesis and cooperate respectfully as one movement, whilst objectively scrutinising our work. We are at an agonising point in human evolution. Yet despite the pain, we have to keep working on whatever scale our lives allow. Collectively, small actions effect big changes, just as the 'big' work of pioneers leads the way for others, so let's celebrate them both.

Last week I was invited to speak to a whole school of children, aged 8 to 13 years old. I give a lot of talks, presentations and workshops, but usually only to adults. I wasn't sure how this one would go. I decided to start off with a YouTube clip: 'Today's Weather Report – Weather girl goes rogue'. It is a spoof TV news programme in which a weather girl recites escalating and increasingly desperate climate change events whilst her news anchor jokes about it being good BBQ weather. Eventually the girl totally loses it and the show is pulled. It is a funny sketch with a serious message. I asked my young audience who was mad: Was it the girl freaking out or the newscaster trying to keep the lid on her? They responded with exactly the right answer: anyone denying climate change is mad.

One thing that really concerns me is our children's future, and their children's and beyond. We are leaving them with a mess, but I don't ever like to present a view of the world that is without hope. I started by arguing that sustainability isn't economic development or growth, but is about the long view. I introduced the Seven Generations Principle, The Great Law of the Iroquois: 'When we plan, make and build, we hold it appropriate to think seven generations ahead. We decide whether the decisions made today will benefit children seven generations into the future.' This worldview can radically change our perspective. It is particularly pertinent to the young.

The rest of my presentation was about ecological solutions. I love telling stories about permaculture and showing photographs of established projects. That day I told them about the WETSystem (Waste Ecological Treatment) at The Sustainability Centre and how Nature and intelligent design can transmute sewage into valuable biomass within what is effectively a zero carbon nature reserve. Fabulous!

I showed them slides about Dr Chris Reij's reforestation work with local people in the Sahel region of Africa, working with little funds and only handtools to build walls that capture sparse rainfall. The Sahel includes Gambia, Senegal, Mauritania, Mali, Niger, Chad, Sudan, Ethiopia, Eritrea and has a combined population of 186 million, the equivalent size of Western Europe. To date, the project has reforested 50,000 square kilometres (21,000 square miles). There are many other projects and innovative people, like Willie Smits and his rainforest restoration work in Borneo. Earth restoration is not a dream; it is a reality. Few of us fully understand Nature's vast regenerative power, but when we work with Nature extraordinary transformations can occur.

After journeying to Africa, we returned home to The Sustainability Centre and I told stories about our work here with children who have never experienced an open fire, let alone cooked over one; who may not have had a positive male role model in their lives; who have not had the opportunity to spend time in Nature … and of the deep healing we witness through the educational programmes run here, so often underfunded, but so important.

I also love to tell stories about Ben Law

and how, when we first acquired the land for the Centre, professional foresters told us that its damaged, overgrown woodland was only worth clearfelling as a paper crop, it had so little value. Ben had a completely different vision and saw the materials for at least five roundwood timber frame buildings on the site. I showed the children our roundwood classroom and explained how Ben built it: with no waste and with the help of apprentices and the community – even our neighbour's grandchildren helped cobble the clay for the cordwood walls.

I was delighted by my young audience's excellent questions: how do WETSystems work? How is water cleansed in natural swimming pools? Why ideally work from edges first when restoring habitats? and so many more … And who, they asked me, are these people who make all this positive and cutting edge media, much of it now online for free, on subjects we never see in the mainstream? We talked about how 'bad news sells newspapers' and I introduced the concept of Transformational Media – how we shape our world by the stories we tell and how vital it is therefore that we tell positive stories. It was evident that these wonderful young people understood all of this and were passionate that 'another world is possible'.

Afterwards, the teachers asked me for my fee and offered to pay my travel expenses. I couldn't take a penny. I felt deeply inspired by the acute intelligence of these children and their questions, and grateful for the opportunity to tell them stories and show slides. I was uplifted and filled with hope for the future. I wanted to give my time as a gift, a moneyless exchange. My generation and our forebears have screwed things up, but I hope that future generations will be far more intelligent and proactive. Let's do whatever we can to inspire them and help them believe that it is still possible to restore the Earth.

Spring emerges after a cold and wet winter in our part of the northern hemisphere. Even in January, the green of snowdrops and bluebells begin to push out through the snow in the woods and in my garden. My heart lifts as the days become longer and I plan the cycle of planting seeds, cleaning and preparing the greenhouse, adding soft fruit to the forest garden, tidying and planting the raised beds … My mind turns to the original and most basic aspects of permaculture, that of providing some of our own home-grown food wherever we live.

As the season changes, I am slowly reading my way through Peter Bane's marvellous treatise, *The Permaculture Handbook*, which is entirely devoted to 'garden farming'. Peter, friend and fellow permaculture publisher, writes of a home-grown self reliance found through taking responsibility for our own household needs as part of a resilient local economy. His book focuses on North America but is replete with detail, years of painstaking research and his own experimentation. The vision in the book is of towns and suburbs being able to provide a significant proportion of food for themselves and the city. I know that this book will be my companion through the next few months.

There are many such examples of garden farming in our recent history. When the Soviet Union collapsed in 1991 with its state-run collective farms in chaos, Peter writes, the peri-urban garden farms were a lifeline for ordinary people, preventing mass hunger. I am not suggesting there will be such a dramatic unravelling in every country, simply that the viability of our economic systems, so dependent on endless growth, is unrealistic and that our industrial food system will flounder. Then modest 'garden farms' will be more than a 'hobby'. Already for some, they make a vital financial contribution to the home budget.

One of the criticisms of permaculture is that it is for people with access to land: for gardeners, smallholders and farmers. What about city people? The team here have been listening and in the last few months we have run some popular online features (just put 'urban' into our search engine on www.permaculture. co.uk) and published two new books, *Permaculture in Pots – how to grow food in small urban spaces* and *Compact Living – how to design small interior space*. The emphasis with both is that by working with what we have, we can grow a proportion of our food, redesign our spaces, simplify our lives and not get caught in the beguiling yet destructive meme of buying larger properties, increasing our mortgages and 'must-have' material possessions and trapping ourselves in even more personal debt. Instead, we have authors Juliet Kemp and Michael Guerra's examples of investing time and energy in growing food, living simply and, in Michael's case, taking his family on wonderful adventures all over Europe by train. He is a passionate advocate of small homes. He asks, "Should we cover the planet with oversized houses, fill the space in between with roads for cars that poison everything, and then export our unsustainable lifestyles to places where there isn't even clean water ..." Check out a great little film he recently made with his family at: http://permanentpublications.co.uk/meet-the-authorsmichael-guerra/

Two other films have really caught my eye recently. One is about guerrilla 'grafters' in California. Tim and I have done a little guerrilla pruning in our own village and harvested the subsequent crop of apples, but how about grafting productive fruiting varieties onto ornamental trees? That's what these guerrillas are doing with just a sharp knife and a little tape. I love this idea. For more details, take a look at: www.permaculture.co.uk/videos/meet-guerrilla-fruit-tree-grafters

Finally, I found this fantastic, funny and inspiring talk given by Mary Clear from Incredible Edible Todmorden, a town in West Yorkshire whose inhabitants were worried about climate change, food security in Africa and their children's future. They decided to turn their town into an edible landscape to make their "community stronger, educate their children in a different way, create jobs and have fun". They are ordinary people, not rich, famous or influential, just ordinary ... They practise the art of 'propaganda gardening' and from their efforts have sprung social enterprises, school gardens, a permaculture training centre, even 'vegetable tourism'! See: www.permaculture.co.uk/ videos/ progaganda-gardening-incredible -edible-todmorden

If you don't own a computer, nip into your local library with this mag, or ask a friend, and have a look. Mary is an

irrepressible force of Nature and she's a real tonic for a weary heart. These ideas – just some of so many – demonstrate that ordinary people, not just a middle class or a wealthy elite, can make a real difference. These ideas alone are not world changing, but they are a burgeoning collective response to poverty, environmental degradation, by becoming more self-reliant and building community resilience ... They inspire me to get outside in all my spare time, grow food, help out at my local community orchard, and support my local community project, The Sustainability Centre. The most important message we can take to heart is that we can indeed make a kinder world and that this isn't altruism. It will in fact make us all more resilient and happier.

Scotland has always held a magical allure for me. As a young child, my mother told me tales of visits to the Outer Hebrides in the early 20th century, places so remote that whale bones lay bleaching on deserted beaches. Aged 14 and incarcerated in a rigid girls' boarding school in Yorkshire, I defiantly ran away and jumped a train bound for Edinburgh. I remember kissing the ground as I stepped onto Scottish soil for the first time. That illicit journey got me into an awful lot of trouble! Afterwards I was to revisit the city for Hogmanay whenever I could, revelling in the joyful abandon of this particularly Scottish celebration. A friend also took me to the Lowlands to a tiny one room croft that had no stairs, simply a ladder to the loft where we slept. I loved the wildness of the place and its simplicity, in such contrast to my city upbringing.

In our twenties and thirties, Tim and I were given the chance to stay in a small croft in the Highlands, tucked away up a small track above Loch Lagan. We collected firewood, checked the water supply that came from a stream straight off the moorland for dead sheep, climbed Ben Nevis and other peaks, and tried our hands at fishing. Most of all, we immersed ourselves in the landscape and stretched our imaginations to its horizons. It was a close thing not to move there, but publishing beckoned and we didn't want to leave our family, all firmly resident down south.

Conferences at Findhorn ecovillage and visits to permaculturists, Graham and Nancy Bell, called us back over the border a few times but I never visited the Hebrides. Then earlier this year friends invited us on a holiday to Iona and we jumped at the chance. Iona, part of the Inner Hebrides, is a small island over the water from Mull, off the west coast. It took two days to drive there and two ferry crossings. I had heard tales of the beauty and the deep peace of the place, once known as 'The Druid Island'. In the 6th century, Columba landed here from Ireland to found a Celtic monastic community.

What joy it is to go somewhere so remote with such wide skies! We walked around the island, admired the Celtic crosses and the Abbey, explored the pristine white sandy beaches and little caves, kayaked in the crystal clear blue sea, foraged for wild garlic, and played (we had a rich mix of generations in our pack). I have always longed to see golden eagles in the wild and trips across to Mull gave us numerous sightings. We even saw a sea eagle. One ferry crossing summed up the whole week. Dolphins had been spotted in the Sound that morning and as we crossed over to Mull a pod of eight swooped and gambolled in the wash of the boat. The whole ferryload of people were enlivened by their effervescent, playful energy. A member of the Ionan Christian community told me that she had never crossed the Sound with a pod before. I told her that I hadn't seen wild dolphins since a visit to Baja, Mexico 25 years ago. "Come to Iona and see dolphins and save your carbon footprint," she replied with a smile.

One recent preoccupation for me has been with wilderness and the deeply healing effect it has on us. I have been working on a book by Glennie Kindred that merges her wonderful insights into the turning of the seasons and ways in which we can mark them with her love of our native and medicinal edibles and herbs and of wild places (see this issue). Our work together has taken us on what Glennie fondly calls 'jaunts' to the wild places in our own locales. Glennie has shown me the splendour of the Peak District with its great caves, collapsed mining shafts that disappear into fathomless depths, gorges, and a mysterious spring that discharges ferrous compounds, opening like a womb in naked intimacy. I have shown her the panoramic views from my beloved South Downs with their tumuli and ancient trackways carpeted by wildflowers in the late spring, and the roar of stags echoing through ancient yew forests in the autumn. We have so enjoyed combining both work and play in such a creative way. Glennie has taught me to relish the wild edge even more and get out into the landscape whatever the weather.

I have also discovered the work of Eleanor O'Hanlon via her book, *The Eyes of the Wild*, which I read word for word avidly. Eleanor writes exquisitely about the Gray Whale, Bear, Wolf and Horse and merges natural history, biology and conservation with insights into shamanism and indigenous cultures from Siberia to North America. This synthesis of deftly woven threads has given me the deepest insights into what could contribute to an emerging permanent culture, one that conserves and celebrates the wild and also, critically for permaculturists, learns from observing wild creatures.

All of my recent immersions in the inner and outer landscape have made it even clearer that through the wonders of Nature and our capacity to see through the 'Eyes of the Wild', we can connect with a consciousness much greater than our little selves. All we need to do is open ourselves and listen. "Diversity is holy. The dazzling play of relationship within the diversity of form is the expression of the inherent sacredness of life," as Eleanor puts it. From this realisation comes a growing capacity to live in harmony with the diversity of all life, and that will hopefully be our salvation.

I want to tell you why permaculture inspires and motivates me and how I apply it in my own life, but before I do that I need to set the scene. Please bear with me.

What do you feel when you read or hear that the Arctic icecap is melting faster than ever before or that clean water, a rapidly dwindling resource, is being globally privatised so that the most vulnerable people will have even less access to it? We are all exposed to these sorts of news reports every day, every time we turn on the TV or radio, or go online. Life is so precious, whether it is animal, human or entire ecosystems, so to see it inexorably damaged (and currently at such an extraordinary rate) makes me feel like a part of me is dying. Our bodies are connected to the great body of the Earth. The destruction of our world is experienced deep in our psyche whether we acknowledge it or not.

Do we switch off, tune out, ease ourselves out of focus in a self-constructed mythology? Many people blinker themselves with their ideas, their politics, their possessions, or their addictions in order to stay disengaged and comfortable. They practise psychological insulation, knowingly or not, especially if they believe the cause is hopeless and that we, the people, are not equipped to fix anything. I don't believe this is the answer. We are here to bear witness to these extraordinary times and to maintain our gaze on the atrocities meted out to other human beings, the other species who share this planet with us and even whole bioregions. We are here to take our place in the world and do what we can

to work towards a peaceful, equitable, more biodiverse and abundant world. We are also here to discover more intelligent and balanced ways of living, and to quietly test them out ourselves. In other words, we cannot ultimately turn away even though it takes great courage to maintain our gaze. This is a naked and vulnerable place to be.

To deal with this, we need to develop our own sense of resilience and the capacity to find balance. Life is not only precious; it is a profound experiment in learning. People often ask me where I draw inspiration from. How do I keep going? I make it my responsibility to be as well informed as I can about the ills of the world and the systems that exact the damage as I can. Then I make it equally my journey to learn more about the solutions: from the grand, inspiring projects that regenerate whole landscapes to the small techniques we can use in our daily life.

It's been a treat to tell stories at various events this year about the great Earth restoration projects undertaken by permaculture people all over the world. I am inspired by the work of Dr Chris Reij who has helped African people in the Sahel region to reforest more than 55,000 hectares of desert that now produces timber, food, medicines and animal fodder (*PM68*).

I will also never forget standing by a lake in Portugal that Sepp Holzer helped construct and watching the early morning mist settle on the banks watering the community's planted fruit and nut trees, and raised vegetable beds. Nature had brought back eagles, otters, ducks and amphibians in response to the reaquification of the landscape, and the dying cork oaks are now starting to grow again. I know that when human beings apply themselves to Earth restoration, Nature responds by regenerating at an exponential rate. It is frankly humbling.

There is an Aboriginal saying, "Big stories are hunting for the right people to tell them." This magazine and its website are a global invitation to you all to share those big stories. We want to express a practical, creative, diverse vision of possibilities for a world which we actively steward rather than destroy. We do not want to forget the little stories, however, so we populate the pages of every issue of this magazine with two types of stories: the great ideas of our time and the small things we can all do. My greenhouse, with its simple irrigation system derived from a 4,000 year old African technology, is an example (see this issue). When the pain of the world chews at my sanity, I seek balance and equanimity from simple things. I believe we humans need to cultivate humility. It is the pathway to true stewardship, so culturally at odds with most of the developed world's history and worldview.

I believe that most people are innately good. Somehow as a collective upon this planet we have lost our way. We have become enthralled by a destructive worldview prosecuted by the very few at the potential expense of our very existence. What I write about here isn't a purely personal exercise in establishing balance or a way of seeking poise in the face of ecolog-

ical breakdown. It is vital that we, together, keep working on the resilient, solutions part of the equation in whatever way we can, even if it feels like most of the world isn't listening. Then, when the majority of people finally wake up to the realities of our destructive impact on this planet, we will be able to offer some of the answers.

> If we do our best to heal the Earth and make our place in her a sustainable one, is there a good chance that we will succeed? Or is it a forlorn hope? It's a big question, and one which can lead to depression if we look at the facts honestly and dispassionately. But to my mind it's the wrong question. Even if we could answer it – and we can never know anything about the future for certain – it would beg the question, How do I want to live my life?
>
> Here I find the teaching of Mahatma Gandhi very useful. One of his precepts was that of non-attachment to the fruits of our labour. All we can do in life is to make sure that we play our own part in it the best way we can. Much as we would like to, we can never do more than that. Everything we do is so complex, and relies for its ultimate completion on so many different people and natural forces, that we can never take responsibility for the final outcome of our actions. We can only take responsibility for our actions themselves.
>
> So my answer to the question, How do I want to live my life? is that I want to be a part of the solution rather than a part of the problem.

**Patrick Whitefield**
*The Earth Care Manual*

# Section Five

# 2013 - 2017

World population is 7.086 billion, by 2017 it reaches 7.523 billion.

**5 December 2013**, Nelson Mandela dies at age 95.

**17 February 2014**, The United Nations Human Rights Council releases a report accusing North Korea of crimes against humanity and compares the regime to that of Nazi Germany.

**13 October 2014**, the British Parliament votes 274-12 to give diplomatic recognition to Palestine.

**11 June 2014**, members of the Islamic State of Iraq and Syria (ISIS) take control of Mosul, in northern Iraq, dealing the government an enormous and unexpected blow. As many as 500,000 people flee Mosul.

**20 July 2015**, Cuba and the US re-establish full diplomatic relations, ending a 54-year stretch of hostility between the nations.

**12 December 2015**, a global climate change pact is agreed at the COP 21 Summit, committing all countries to reduce carbon emissions for the first time, but many worry that it is too little and too late.

**23 June 2016**, Brexit: the United Kingdom votes in a referendum to leave the European Union.

**3 September 2016**, the US and China, together responsible for 40% of the world's carbon emissions, both formally joined the global Paris Agreement on climate change.

**9 September 2016**, the government of North Korea conducts its fifth and reportedly biggest nuclear test.

**23 December 2016**, the United Nations Security Council adopts Resolution 2334 condemning "Israeli settlements in Palestinian territories occupied since 1967".

**21 January 2017**, millions of people worldwide join the Women's March in response to the inauguration of Donald Trump. 420 marches were reported in the US and 168 in other countries, becoming the largest single-day protest in American history and the largest worldwide protest in recent history.

In the permaculture world, the International Permaculture Conference (IPC) is held at Friends House in London. It is followed by a Convergence near London. I go to my first IPC! 1,200 attend between the conference and convergence from over 70 countries. There are 30 edge events, including a social permaculture course held at The Sustainability Centre with Looby Macnamara, Peter Cow, Starhawk, Robin Clayfield and Robina McCurdy. IPC12 itself consists of over 150 workshops and 26 scholarships are funded, enabling people to attend from many different countries. It's great to meet up with friends and make new ones too. I am particularly delighted to meet Robyn Francis from Australia at last.

IPC is followed in 2016 with a European Convergence in Italy on the shores of Lake Bolsena in an exquisite medieval town of that name. Tim and I attend and are charmed by the beauty of Tuscany, the warmth of Italian hospitality, and ancient Etruscan history.

Permanent Publications publishes numerous books during this time. One of the most mainstream is the *No Dig Organic Home and Garden* by Charles Dowding and Stephanie Hafferty which takes first place on a well-known online store for weeks. We also release more YouTubes and use social media to get the message out daily. We see other publishers like New Society and Storey start releasing permaculture books.

In the Harlands' world, Gail decides to go to university to study Marine and Natural History Photography. Her final projects are about the effects of agriculture on climate and biodiversity and the remediative possibilities of carbon sequestration through regenerative agriculture. She says that focusing on practical solutions helps her deal with the bleak reality of escalating climate change. Hayley becomes a professional singer/songwriter and settles in London and has a garden. One weekend, helping her plant veg and prune shrubs, I discover that she has made some excellent compost the preceding year. Together we mulch beds with it.

Though both our daughters are very much their own people, they both share our passion for the Earth and concern for people, especially the vulnerable. They are spirited and principled women and Tim and I are naturally very proud of them. This generation has it far tougher than any post-war generation. I love to see the next generation of permaculturists emerging. How has their upbringing influenced them? What will they do with their lives? How will they make a difference?

At *PM*, we have always actively worked with young people, but as publishing undergoes a revolution, it becomes even more relevant to do so. Younger people are digital natives and they pick up skills quickly. They bring energy, vision, a capacity for honesty and good critical faculties. We want to run an organisation that is self-responsible and able to quickly adapt. Secondly, we want to teach them communication and publishing skills so that they can take our work forward. We are concerned with succession. So this period of our lives is about beginning to design in succession and look towards a future where Tim and I are no longer lynch pins that hold the work together. Again, we are exploring another edge, trying to step back and become slowly less essential to the publishing company's day-to-day survival.

This is an intensely frustrating and anxious time for those who are worried about climate change. Earlier this year we hit 400 parts per million (ppm) of $CO_2$ in the atmosphere for the first time in human existence. $CO_2$ levels haven't been this high for 4.5 million years and it looks like we may have a rise in global temperature of 6ºC by 2100. I am not going to describe what this means in detail but this is a world with no polar ice caps and sea levels 40 metres higher. The sane response would be to do everything to curb atmospheric $CO_2$. I am frankly afraid of how insane our current behaviour is.

Bert Harvey recently told me an African proverb: 'Calm seas do not make skilled sailors'. We will, by the power of Nature, be forced to become more skilled not only as 'mariners' but also in our articulation of these coming changes and methods of adaptation. I pray that we will also change our ways and I have spent years thinking about how that process of change is initiated.

Beyond publishing this magazine and our books, our work touches other spheres and allows us to explore change. We are lucky to be part of a community, a former Royal Navy base that is now The Sustainability Centre. The centre is an educational charity founded in 1995 and I am currently the Chair of the Board of Trustees. My voluntary work here brings even greater engagement with others and balance into my life. It is an instructive process.

Many wonderful things happen at The Sustainability Centre. We run a campsite and ecolodge, and welcome around 20,000 adult visitors here a year, whether they drop in for a cup of tea, take a course or stay here. We also run the South Downs Natural Burial Site which this year was voted the best site in the UK by the people who had need of these services. This is a big accolade and the guys who do this work are deeply dedicated. They help families in difficult circumstances whilst running the site to the highest ecological standards; people feel a connection and sense of investment in the Centre. Some return and volunteer on projects and form tight-knit groups who regularly work together. Working here, I get to watch a barren, overstood conifer plantation transforming into a biodiverse broadleaf woodland, and scrubland returning to chalk downland, alive with insects, reptiles, mammals and birds. From grief springs new hope.

Three thousand school children also visit the Centre every year: residential schools attending our South Downs Experience week, children coming to a day event or course, plus a special six week programme for children who are 'failing' at school. They may have special needs and find the conventional academic curriculum irrelevant, or they may have experienced a trauma in the family and are desperately unhappy. They spend time outside doing practical work, learning new skills rather than being confined in a room, segregated from their peers. Our education team teach them bushcraft, food growing and outdoor cooking, forestry and forest school skills. You could be forgiven for raising an eyebrow when the unruly are taught how to sharpen blades or to make fire from a spark, but what is really cultivated here is trust, respect, hope and a real love of the outdoors. From feeling academically useless, some of these kids go on to college and take practical courses. Others simply start smiling again. One girl told me that her desperation was so great she didn't want to live anymore. Her time at the Centre literally saved her life. All of these stories deeply move me.

Some of our schools are from desperately poor areas and struggle to find funds to come here. A recent inner city school gave us an insightful experience. Whilst out in the woods, one child asked, "Am I in a rainforest, miss?" The only frame of reference she had was from a lesson about the Amazon Rainforest. The class had no concept of their own local ecology, something that should be every child's heritage. We believe that "We will not fight to save what we do not love and we cannot love what we do not know." (Stephen Jay Gould.)

Our aim is to teach and inspire through 'immersion'. We want our visitors, young and old, to be immersed in the values, ecology, technology and society of our Centre and come away refreshed and enlivened by it. I recently taught a session at a Permaculture Design Course here. My parting words were: "Never think it is all over and that adaptation is our only route. Choose a life that is creative and responsive to change. Be practical and realistic but never give up. Standing behind you is an entire global network of people who are supporting you."

At the beginning of spring I look out over the garden and see our no dig veggie beds, weed free and mulched with homemade compost, the fruit trees pruned and new trees planted adding to the forest garden. The snowdrops have pushed through the frost and the birdsong has intensified telling me the birds are nest building. As I watch the natural world regenerate in this wonderful seasonal cycle, I feel inspiration and hope rising within me like sap.

Recently, my eldest daughter and I walked in the woods and visited a special beech tree that is over 300 hundred years old. Its branches were pollarded long ago, possibly to mark a field boundary, and now its huge limbs reach up beyond the canopy into the sky. We have been visiting this tree for 27 years, longer than both our daughters' lives. Someone carved a heart on the trunk years ago and we named it The Heart Tree, but that too is disappearing as the bark develops over time. My daughter told me that whenever she walks in the woods she visits the tree. I like to think of this continuity, of the values Tim and I may have engendered in our children. However far they travel in the world, they still come home to this special tree. We must celebrate its calm presence whilst it is still standing. Many ancient giants have fallen due to an unusually wet and stormy winter brought to us across the Atlantic by an oscillating jet stream.

# 79 | Spring 2014

The weather has made me think a lot about my garden and the food we grow. It is hard to predict the last frosts, the hail in spring that destroys fruit tree blossom, or a wet summer, as in 2012, that rotted crops in the ground. In response, I have started to grow as much as I can under glass and we are developing microclimates in the forest garden whilst still leaving enough space for as much light as possible. Food forests are wonderful but we have to be careful so far from the Equator not to weaken our trees and shrubs by cramming too many together in naive optimism.

We don't only grow perennials – much though I love the diversity we can achieve, the fabulous blossom, the resilience of established edible perennials and the experience of foraging in our own wilderness – we like annuals too. Hence our visit to Charles Dowding's organic no dig market garden (see this issue). There is no better learning than to observe a truly experienced gardener (or farmer). They know what works through years of observation, trial and error. Charles inspired me and encouraged us to plant more annual varieties as well as perennials, experiment with at least two new crops every year, and be prepared to be challenged by the weather.

In a rapidly changing world, resilience occupies my mind … David Holmgren, the co-founder of permaculture, has been raising unpalatable questions in his recent paper, 'Crash on Demand – Welcome to the Brown Tech Future' (2013, http://holmgren.com.au/crash-demand). It is an update on his book, *Future*

*Scenarios* (2009) and his paper 'Oil vs Money – Battle for Control of the World' (2009). It has sparked an online debate that has engaged many commentators in the permaculture, transition and environmental activism movements. Is David a 'Collapsnik' actively encouraging a crash to avert an even greater global disaster, namely runaway climate change? Or is he simply commentating on what that crash may look like if it occurs, and how positive environmental movements (like permaculture and transition) can engage others in constructive resilience building strategies?

David MacLeod wrote (on www.resilience.org) a useful appraisal of the debate and a summary of David's underlying philosophy. This first appeared in *Permaculture One* (1978), was concluded in his essay 'Energy and Permaculture' (1998), and appears again in this recent paper. So where do we start? Here is David's code to live by:

- Reduce, Reuse, Recycle (in that order)
- Grow a garden and eat what it produces
- Avoid imported resources where possible
- Use labour and skill in preference to materials and technology
- Design, build and purchase for durability and repairability
- Use resources for their greatest potential use (e.g. electricity for tools and lighting, food scraps for animal feed)
- Use renewable resources wherever possible even if local environmental costs appear

higher (e.g. wood rather than electricity for fuel and timber rather than steel for construction)

- Use non-renewable and embodied energies primarily to establish sustainable systems (e.g. passive solar housing, food gardens, water storage, forests)
- When using high technology (e.g. computers) avoid using state of the art equipment
- Avoid debt and long-distance commuting
- Reduce taxation by earning less
- Develop a home-based lifestyle; be domestically responsible.

I do not anticipate with pleasure the chaos and suffering an economic crash will bring to ordinary people's lives. I doubt David does either. What I appreciate is David's thoughtful capacity to project into the future and offer a code to live by for a positive and unifying response.

At the end of a long winter, Tim and I took a road trip to the West Country. First stop was Sidcot Quaker School, where I spent the last years of my school life. I had been invited to speak there. I feel an urgency to talk with young people about the challenges they face, and also the solutions. This is not to sugar coat the bitter pills of over population, climate change and the devastation of irresponsible techno-fixes like tar sand extraction and fracking … As a society we rarely tell the positive, inspiring and life-changing stories in any depth and it is vital that the next generation has the opportunity to hear both the realities of life on our planet and that there are genuinely innovative people and projects throughout the world.

After school came visits to two very different farms. We spent the day with Tim Mead of Yeo Valley Farms, a large organic dairy business that produces millions of units of product a year. Tim explained how he farms organically on this scale. He told us about the rotation system that produces organic feed for his cows (silage, crimped wheat and other cereals) and seasonal grazing (a mix of grass and clover), the scale of the composting systems (long windrows that border the fields) and how the distribution business is run in the most efficient way possible. We also met one of his prize bulls and learnt about their breeding programme, developed over decades to produce healthy, productive British Friesians. As an independent, organic mainstream business, Yeo Valley hold a UK market share as big as the vast

multinational, Danone. Whilst their farming model is far from small scale and local, they are fiercely independent. We also noted the dedication and enthusiasm of Yeo Valley staff and the pride and attention to detail both on the farm and at their HQ.

Our next stop in south Devon couldn't have been a greater contrast. We were visiting Rebecca Hosking and her business partner, Tim Green, on their new 175 acre farm they very recently moved on to. You may remember Rebecca and Tim made a 'Farm For The Future', a BBC documentary about Peak Oil, climate change, permaculture, agroforestry and the future of farming (see article also in *PM60*). Since then they have experimented with soil building and carbon sequestering regenerative agriculture techniques on Rebecca's family farm. Last winter (the wettest in England and Wales since records began in 1766) was a real test of their work. She told me, "People are finally realising that how we manage and farm the land affects not only how much carbon is released but also how much we can sequester. Similarly how much water, which once washed off our fields, is now being absorbed. In just 18 months of soil building we noticed the herb and grass regrowth dramatically speed up and increase in density, all the time acting as a large carbon sink."

The real eye-opener for them was the clarity and low flow levels of water leaving their land compared to that of their neighbours. "By implementing simple money saving land management changes we have seen dramatic results which are now not just benefiting us but others around us. Imagine if many other farms were to do this, we'd see a high reduction in floods and all of us sequestering carbon to build fertility."

Rebecca and Tim practised mob grazing with sheep, fertilising pasture with compost teas, laying old boundary hedges, repairing dry stone walls and planting top fruit, nut trees and edible shrubs on the margins of grazing areas. Re-establishing a more mixed ecology and mimicking Nature by mob grazing with animals kickstarted the farm into a regenerative state, building soil, improving the sward, augmenting animal health, creating greater biodiversity and, significantly, absorbing rainwater into the land.

In March this year they moved to a new farm of their own to test out their techniques on a larger scale. We wanted to see the land (overgrazed, compacted, with little top soil and hedges almost flailed to the point of extinction) before they set to work and to meet their hardy flock of sheep (Shetlands crossed with Nordic – an arresting and unconventional sight in south Devon!). These sheep produce lambs with little difficulty, can survive on arable weeds and pasture without additional feeds, and are ideal to kickstart the ecology of the land. They have beautiful fleeces and produce tasty cuts of meat with no inputs. Rebecca and Tim graze the flock in small areas and move them daily, avoiding compaction or over grazing ... and all without

a sheep dog. Rebecca explained, "If you are gentle and never shout at them, the flock will follow a bucket of sheep nuts." 120 biddable sheep is quite a sight! You will hear more of this landmark regenerative agriculture project in the future.

Last stop was a visit to Rob Hopkins, the co-founder of the Transition Movement, in Totnes. We have known Rob for some years and so it was great to catch up. What I love most about him is his lightness of being. Though he writes some of the best contemporary commentaries on climate change, he retains a sense of humour.* I asked him if we could run an April Fool by him on permaculture.co.uk and he had no hesitation. It made me smile for days. Maintaining a sense of joy in life is for me an essential ingredient of survival.

---

* www.transitionnetwork.org/blogs/rob-hopkins

# 83 | Spring 2015

Some years ago, Tim and I were walking on a hot, dry day in the Himalayas to find a monastery in the Punakha District in Bhutan. Located near Lobesa, it stands on a round hillock and was built in 1499 by the 14th Drukpa hierarch, Ngawang Choegyel. The 'Divine Madman', maverick saint Drukpa Kunley (1455-1529), had previously blessed the site and built a chorten there. I have a soft spot for this Divine Madman. Instead of trying to teach his followers the Buddhist Way with protracted meditation, abstinence and scholarship, he chose singing, jokes and outrageous behaviour, saying that divine knowledge was not governed by rules. He is also the saint who advocated the use of phallus symbols as paintings on walls and flying carved wooden phalluses on house tops at the four corners of the eves, but I digress …

We crossed paddy fields and walked uphill in the heat, arriving at this monastery near a small agricultural village. There on the hillside was a little, but perfect, forest garden, a layered polyculture of annual and perennial fruits and vegetables with all the crops adequately spaced to take advantage of the sunlight, but also with the benefit of shade in the dry heat of the day. Each niche in the layers was optimised for plant health and yields. I had of course read that Robert Hart, who brought forest gardening to Britain in the 1970s and '80s, was inspired by the forest gardens of Kerala in India. So here I was seeing a Bhutanese version, evolved through observation of Nature, experience and common sense.

Permaculturists can spend rather a lot of time trying to explain what permaculture is and I am no different. In many ways it is rather a difficult word, a concept that is alien to our post-industrial Western society. What we can forget to do is to attribute its origins. It was not really 'invented' by two Australians, Bill Mollison and David Holmgren, in a bolt of enlightenment. I believe it evolved, and was coded from, protracted study of perennial systems in agroforestry, tree cropping, Yeoman's keylining and specifically Bill's interaction with, and observation of, Aboriginal and other indigenous peoples and their practices wherever he travelled. These ways of observing and working with Nature are the legacy and heritage of indigenous peoples all over the globe. They do not call it permaculture. They have often not heard the word, yet they understand Nature's patterns and use them to create polycultural, perennially based, energy efficient homes, gardens, farms, communities … These are found all over the world where remnants of those cultures have been allowed to survive. They deserve acknowledgement and respect.

So no one actually 'invented' permaculture. Good ideas and good practices have been borrowed from indigenous cultures. These have been mixed with appropriately scaled renewable technologies and low embodied energy materials to try and design the most ecologically elegant solutions to our current problems: pollution, excessive consumption of resources, tools and practices that rely on mechanisation driven by fossil fuels.

This is a big year for permaculture with

many events and conferences happening in the world. This is especially so for the UK, as we are hosting the next International Permaculture Conference and Convergence in and near London. The Permaculture Association (Britain), our educational charity, wants to make this event as open and inclusive as possible. They have actively sought funds for bursaries to enable people from all over the world to attend. They do not want to host a gathering only for people who can afford it. Their aspiration is to create opportunities for all delegates to share knowledge and information, respectfully and from diverse cultures.

In a world of escalating racial tension and conflict, I believe it is time for the permaculture movement to open its eyes and actively support a process that acknowledges and respects its legacy from indigenous people. We are all unconsciously conditioned by our colour and our upbringing. I had thought I was a pretty liberal and educated white woman, but now I understand that there are parts to my psyche that are hidden from me – my 'privilege' – a second skin I barely see. There are therefore experiences that I will never have and probably never fully understand, however much I educate myself.

For the permaculture movement to grow, we have to face our personal and cultural limitations and open our eyes to them. We also need to understand our countries' unvarnished histories, acknowledge our differences as well as our similarities, and appreciate the indigenous legacy that permaculture thinking has appropriated and taken as its own. If we can do this, we begin a journey towards a more genuinely polycultural movement. This must be a movement of humility and respect – one that of course abhors all violence and extremism – but not one that uses satire and factionalism in the name of free speech. Instead, we need to learn to place our solidarity in peace, co-operation and the humble desire to learn and grow.

In the rural Shona African community in Zimbabwe, five villages of 7,000 people have joined together to form the Chikukwa Project, named after their local chief. Twenty years ago their land was deforested, barren and nothing would grow there in the summer months. When the rains came, they washed down the slopes taking the soil with them. The springs had dried up and the people were poor, hungry and suffering from malnutrition.

The Shona decided to do something about it and sought advice from permaculture pioneer, John Wilson. Slowly, a field at a time, they built water retaining landscapes: terracing the slopes and digging swales to hold the water in the soil. They added composted manure to these terrace beds to build soil and grow food. They stopped grazing animals and foraging for firewood in the gullies where the springs rose and planted native trees there to hold the moisture in the soil. They also stopped untethered grazing of goats on the hillsides, allowing trees to regenerate, and they started driving their cattle to agreed grazing areas. They learnt new skills: specifically permaculture training, conflict resolution, women's empowerment, primary education and HIV management.

Within three years, the springs began to reactivate. They saw that the yields from the plots with swales were bigger than the plots without them. Twenty years later,

where there was once eroded soil and overgrazed slopes, there are now reforested gullies with flowing water, terraces full of vegetables, grains and fruit, and high ridges lined with trees for firewood. In the villages, there are home gardens, pens for hens and goats, water tanks to catch rainfall run-off, and a culture of co-operation that values people skills as much as horticultural techniques. The landscape is verdant and biodiverse, and the gardens and farms produce crops for the families and for market, bringing an economic yield back into the region. All this in one generation.

Film makers, Gillian and Terrence Leahy, were invited to make a film about this transformation at Chikukwa.* They saw how these Shona Africans had pulled themselves out of hunger and malnutrition, using permaculture farming techniques and bottom-up social organisation. They understood that this could be replicated anywhere in the world.

The Loess Plateau in China, an area the size of France, was similarly regenerated using water retention landscapes. This was documented by John D. Liu in his incredible film, 'Green Gold'.** There are many more stories from all over the world where permaculture and other regenerative techniques have been applied to barren lands. Earth restoration is not only possible, it is already happening. We need to build capacity and find ways to take this

---

* To learn more about this project and see the film, visit: www.thechikukwaproject.com
** See the film at: www.permaculture.co.uk/videos/green-goldhow-can-we-regenerate-large-scale-damaged-ecosystems

work wherever it is needed, helping people to lift themselves out of poverty and rebuild broken communities. John calls this 'the great work of our time', work that not only restores whole ecosystems but also brings dignity and wellbeing to our fellow human beings. Nelson Mandela said, "Overcoming poverty is not a task of charity, it is an act of Justice. Like slavery and apartheid, poverty is not natural. It is man made and can be overcome and eradicated by the actions of human beings. Sometimes it falls on a generation to be great. You can be that generation. Let greatness blossom."

It is perhaps easier to regenerate rural landscapes where the vestiges of a traditional culture retain gardening and farming skills, but it can happen in post-industrial wastelands too. I have been following permaculture teacher, Sarah Pugh, as she travels through the urban American landscape, researching urban permaculture projects. Sarah lives in Bristol, UK and works with permaculture and transition there. She set up Shift Bristol, a training project that takes people through a year of learning practical permaculture. Sarah wanted, however, to reach beyond her own city and see for herself what urban regeneration looks like in places like Detroit, Chicago and San Francisco where the extremes of wealth and poverty are keenly experienced. She visited Detroit and observed, "So much space, so much energy, so many problems ... so much potential. The population of Brightmoor [a local neighbourhood] has dropped from 20,000 to less than 10,000. 70,000 empty, burned out and rotting houses in Detroit. Community gardening in full swing here ..."

Sarah leaves a trail of hope on social media as she travels. It is such a different story from the usual diet of pet videos, celebrity gossip and the haunting escalation of our global problems. We hear too much of the dark side in all media, and too little of the solutions. I am convinced that it makes people turn away and disengage, feeling that our futures are hopelessly predetermined.

# 85 | Autumn 2015

We recently launched a series of films, 'Living With The Land', about permaculture in the garden, on the farm, on a rural smallholding, in the city, and in community – with film makers, Permaculture People, Phil Moore and Lauren Simpson.* We wanted this series to seed permaculture ideas outside our 'community', so we asked well-known people like Kevin McCloud, Sir Tim Smit, Bruce Parry and expert Colin Tudge to introduce them. The idea is to engage a wider audience in permaculture and to flag up the International Permaculture Conference and Convergence that is happening this September in the UK.

With all the bad and sad news in the world, we want to get a real buzz going about the many good people and projects that are happening around the world and how low cost, simple practices can transform whole landscapes. It is with some pleasure therefore that I also welcome John D. Liu as a writer to this issue. John has been filming Earth restoration projects for years (see this issue) and ably articulates the longing in many of us: to place our energies in healing and restoring the Earth and to make redundant the ecological, economic and social paradigms that drive poverty, scarcity, inequality, habitat destruction and species collapse. These techniques and technologies are proven. We are just waiting to be heard.

At the end of our third 'Living With The Land' film about regenerative agriculture, Rebecca Hosking sums up the joy of this approach: "What I love about permaculture, from a wildlife background, is the ecology in it. It is working with ecology – it is not viewing us separate from ecology – we have our place within the web. We are working with the elements ... permaculture makes you study, observe and question, and you are forever learning. We have the most amazing teacher, dear old Mother Nature. If I have five more lifetimes, I am never going to learn all her secrets, but every single day I come away and say, 'I didn't know that. That's fascinating!' I just want to learn, it keeps me alive and really makes me appreciate the world."

This engaged, joyful way of working with Nature is a powerful, regenerative praxis. It is all too human to become overwhelmed by the human-induced problems of the world and believe that they are insurmountable. Problems become like edifices that society believes can never crumble. Yet I ask you to think of examples of situations or elements in our collective life that have unexpectedly changed. As a small child, I vividly recall the invasion of Czechoslovakia in 1968 when Soviet tanks rumbled into the beautiful, medieval capital city, Prague. I can still hear the description on the BBC News. It seemed impossible then that the Berlin Wall would collapse by 1989, yet it did – because the system was completely dysfunctional. Our current economic system, so addicted to growth for its survival, is heading that way, causing dangerous levels of carbon dioxide,

* www.permaculture.co.uk/living-with-the-land

widespread habitat collapse and the sixth mass extinction. Many of us who have been predicting this for decades have been received sceptically, often with ridicule. Vested interests create powerful social memes and those who argue this is not happening are as convincing as cigarette manufacturers of the 1950s who claimed smoking does not cause cancer.

Rebecca's perspective about lifelong learning and happiness touches me. Nature is a force far greater than ourselves and is a willing and powerful teacher. If you have ever been at the epicentre of a storm, as I was recently, you will know that your little life hangs by a thread. All our human endeavours pale into insignificance in the face of Nature's power. In life, we need to slow down, immerse ourselves deeply in her rhythms, and observe over long periods of time. This process, with research and study, expands our narrow perspective and helps us to develop new muscles, both mental and physical. Nature shows us the scope of our lives, who we really are, and teaches us humility and wisdom.

*In the course of history, there comes a time*
*when humanity is called to shift to a new*
*level of consciousness, to reach a higher moral*
*ground. A time when we have to shed our fear*
*and give hope to each other. That time is now.*

WANGARI MAATHAI

In September 2015 I attended my first
International Permaculture Conference
and Convergence. I have never had the
opportunity before, for various reasons,
such as a reluctance to spend carbon on
flying and financial constraints. Both the
Conference and then the Convergence
were in the UK and were attended by
over 1,200 people from over 70 countries.
Both events were feats of organisation by
the Permaculture Association (Britain),
our national networking charity, and
involved wall-to-wall opportunities to
attend workshops about every aspect of
permaculture. I came away deeply inspired
by the hardworking, noble and unselfish people I met who work tirelessly on
projects at the cutting edge of innovation.
I learned about ecosystem restoration,
delved deep into soil science, growing food
forests, permaculture's response to climate
change, the refugee crisis, social and racial
equality, alternative income sharing … so
many subjects, so much expertise, and all
presented from a perspective of practice
rather than theory. I also experienced
a sense of optimism and camaraderie that
only face to face contact can offer, and I felt

blessed. I enjoyed giving my presentations
too, especially telling the story of my forest
garden, from barren, silent arable field to
a productive edible landscape teeming with
biodiversity and food.

Like any movement, the permaculture
world is subject to criticism. We are accused
of being unscientific, so the recent launch
of the Permaculture International Research
Network* will encourage a growing vigour
to document and test the science behind
permaculture design. We are planning to
launch a peer reviewed journal with an
international editorial board, supported
by universities and research institutes
from at least four continents, to encourage
the publication of permaculture research
and practice.

We are also subject to self-criticism and
are aware that the more visible teachers,
authors and leaders of the movement tend
to still be white, male Westerners and we
are seeking ways of becoming more racially
and socially inclusive. In multi-racial societies, how many people of colour hold the
highest offices? How many countries in the
world currently have a female head of state/
prime minister? Currently, 22 out of 196.**
How many countries place environmental
protection before GDP? These questions
are uncomfortable but they have to be
asked. Nations governed by indigenous
people, such as Bolivia, have set an example
to the industrialised nations who are held
in the sway of ecocidal corporate interests.

* www.permaculture.org.uk/research/4-international-research-network
** www.jjmccullough.com/charts_rest_female-leaders.php

Becoming more inclusive requires education and a growing awareness of our own conditioning. It is a painfully slow process. We live in a patriarchal world where old colonial ambition still holds sway in either subtle or completely overt and brutal ways. The permaculture movement is trying to move beyond this conditioning, but it has some way to go. This shift needs to be at the core of permaculture. The Black Permaculture Network is eloquent: "We are committed to envision, design and create a world in which we affirm and celebrate human diversity, where we can learn from one another's perspectives and support one another's struggles. We are proud to lend our support to all those who work to make that vision real."* Co-operation and harmony are the keys to human survival, not violence, racism, sectarianism, elitism and war-mongering. At *PM* we believe we must speak up for those who are oppressed and excluded. We need to model the change we want to see in the world.

---

* http://blackpermaculturenetwork.org/solidarity-statement

A friend of mine recently asked me what makes my heart sing. My mind's eye immediately travelled to an estuary on the west coast of Ireland. Here, on the incoming tide at sunset, the heron hunts for prey in the shallows, terns dive for small fish, and the occasional seal or dolphin languidly swims into the bay.

When the mackerel are running in late August, huge shoals of these beautiful, iridescent pelagic fish drive sprats into the estuary which leap from the water in the dance of predator and prey. It feels like the whole landscape is potentised by Life itself.

I feel the same as I walk in the woodlands on the English South Downs. There, beech hundreds of years old and the occasional yew and holly are mixed with overgrown hazel coppice and ash. I can see the old ways of pollarding trees for fuel and animal fodder in their shapes and the neglected stools of coppice, once cut in seven year cycles for crafts and charcoal, waiting to be brought back into rotation. In winter, if I am lucky, I will catch the oyster mushrooms fruiting in a cold snap on the beech. Early in the new year, there is emerging evidence of the carpet of bluebells yet to come, followed soon by the blooms of celandine, wood anemone, primrose and then the ancient woodland indicator, 'Town Hall Clock' (*Adoxa moschatellina*). I dream of a time when ecosystems are restored and every niche is filled with no missing links, no gaps left by the absence of predator or prey. This is Life in its abundant cycle – in a state

of balance, in a state of grace – the 'rewilding' dream. Recently I have started to understand how we can help this happen, and incredibly it can happen on the farm.

Rebecca Hosking recently wrote an online article* describing how Village Farm in Devon, where she and four colleagues are pushing the boundaries of regenerative agriculture, is more than a farm in the conventional sense. It is an ecosystem with a mixture of wild and domesticated species: "… to keep the domestic species healthy and happy we need the wild ones … giving equal importance to all because, as we all know, to have a healthy ecosystem you need great abundance and diversity of life," she writes. We are a species that can cohabit the land rather than strip it of resources. Better than that, Rebecca says we can act as a 'keystone species' and replace the ecological benefits of an animal that is locally extinct (like the beaver, eagle, lynx or wolf).** "A keystone plays a crucial role in maintaining the structure of an ecological community, affecting many other creatures in an ecosystem." Keystone species are usually predators that we have eliminated and are usually at the top of the food chain, regulating the species below them and therefore having a profound effect on their surroundings. "We, like the beaver, can dig ponds, create streams and slow water down, allowing it to penetrate the soil. We can and are working currently like a wolf; our form of grazing called 'Holistic Planned Grazing' means we move our flock around

* www.permaculture.co.uk/articles/wild-farm-regenerative-agriculture-village-farm
** A concept first proposed by ecologist and farmer, Tim Green (1974-2017), at Village Farm.

our land as if they were on migration. Suddenly from herbivores (namely sheep in our case) damaging the soil and creating greenhouse gases, our sheep become part of a symbiotic relationship that locks down carbon and builds topsoil, a system that's worked for millions of years."

The lynx, she says, pushes herbivores away from wooded areas allowing woodland to re-establish. Gardeners and farmers can also have the same effect as smaller animals planting nuts like jays and squirrels, sowing seeds like song birds and encouraging wild flowers to flourish through our management of cutting or grazing. To me, this idea is deeply insightful. I can now see the pattern behind regenerative agriculture and understand why these techniques are so effective. In my own small way as a gardener, I am the lynx that enables the trees to grow, the beaver who dams, creating ponds, the songbird who sows seeds, the squirrel who buries nuts ... I am a part of the land, rather than its steward. I have always felt this intuitively, but the crew at Village Farm have given me an ecological context. They show how we can become a force for good, holding a niche until the time comes for the keystone species to reinhabit an ecosystem, at the same time still growing food, fodder, fuel and medicines. This is why we are here at this time and this is a dream that makes my heart sing.

Last night I had a dream. I was flying over a landscape and as I looked down I saw a lake. I could see the shoreline with beaches and inlets. There, at every place where the slope up from the water to dry land was gentle and sandy, a huge fish as long as my body was emerging.

I wanted to look more closely at these large muscular creatures. As I dived down I saw that they were attempting to use their fins to ease their bodies out of the water onto the land. This was not an easy step, rather an exploration of risk. Their scaley forms were not adapted to the land, nor their gills to the air, yet they were endeavouring to face the danger and survive a different medium. I could sense their vulnerability and fear, yet the allure of the land and its new potential was more powerful. There was an imperative to take the risk.

What will it take for humans to take the next evolutionary step? It will not be the colonisation of a far planet. Our evolution is not about switching habitats or respiratory mediums, and it is more subtle than a matter of physical risk and courage. We need to change the story of *Homo sapiens*, the story that tells us that our whole biology is based on fight or flight, on competition and not co-operation.

Darwin has been given some bad press about the survival of the fittest and there has been a distortion of his ideas in relation to the human species. Industrialists like Andrew Carnegie have sold us an economic meme that we have to fight each other and dominate all the other species on this planet in order to survive. The opposite is true. The more we stockpile wealth, wage war (a very expensive and profitable export business for developed nations), persecute the more vulnerable (our fellow humans and other species) with our weaponry of dominance, the more we impoverish ourselves, our cultures and our fundamental capacity for compassion. Darwin's book, *The Descent of Man*, argued that the human species had succeeded because of traits like sharing and compassion. "Those communities," he wrote, "which included the greatest number of the most sympathetic members would flourish best, and rear the greatest number of offspring."

The avarice of survival's ugly colours has been exposed in the rich of the world's preference to populate offshore funds in tax havens rather than contribute to the building blocks of society – welfare, education, health care, preservation of natural resources and so on – leaving this responsibility to the less affluent and the poor's meagre pockets. This is more than a sociopathic disconnection from our own shared humanity, it is also the abnegation of our deep interconnection with all species. Our political elite and their dark practices are coming to light.

There have always been people throughout history who have turned their backs on fear-driven materialism, ideologies of war and unconscionable greed. We have recognised them as prophets, avatars and great leaders. The next evolutionary step for humanity is to debunk the myth of aggression and competition being the imperative of survival. The next step is to haul our maladapted psychologies out of the muddy waters of fear and austerity and into a lighter, more expansive realm of compassion. This is a powerful response in a brutal world. It comes from a deep understanding of our shared humanity and our place in the web of all species.

I do not think permaculture is the answer to all our ills – it has its shortcomings and blind spots – but I do see it as a framework that has the potential to gather together useful techniques, technologies and ideas, and organise them coherently. For me, every article in this issue demonstrates this intelligent coherence: the education of children away from the ubiquitous 'screen'; a positive relationship between developed world enterprise and fair trade in the Global South; the huge capacity to lock up carbon in agroecological systems (carbon farming) and thereby create a potent approach to tackling climate change; simple, clever, small solutions and technologies; food, health and unusual crops; and 'growing' people too. All the people in this magazine are voices of this [r]evolutionary movement and together I hear a growing song that is being sung all over the world.

Fins out of the water everyone?

What does permaculture have to do with politics? The original contraction of permanent agriculture to permaculture is also the contraction of permanent culture. Having identified perennial systems (treecrops and agroforestry, for example) as vital techniques to restore ecosystems, co-originators, Bill Mollison and David Holmgren, quickly turned their attention to the ethics of earth care, people care and limits to growth/sharing surplus. It is evident that permaculture is more than a design system or ecotoolkit as its essence is nested in an ethical worldview.

How can we then have a permanent culture – one in which there is freedom of speech, intellectual vigour, diversity of opinions and worldviews, and an economic base that embraces the triple bottom line – planet and people before profit – in a neoliberal economic world designed to put profit before anything else? We cannot. Permaculture may not be a political movement but it cannot put its head in the sand and say that it has nothing to do with developing an alternative to neo-Keynesian economics that is raping the planet's ecosystems and impoverishing the vast majority of its people. We have to stand back from our current economic and political systems and seek true democracy. Otherwise we will quickly destroy what is left of our home and ourselves with it.

A huge impediment to our imagination is that we live in a world where media shapes our thoughts. From kindergarten,

we are selected to succeed based on our malleability to fit in with the predominant system. The mainstream media is a vehicle designed to advance the causes of those who own and run it. There is a monopoly of wealth and power in our society which translates directly into a monopoly of the media. The result is a dangerous lack of diversity and pluralism of voices and opinions in the mainstream space. The media has become little more than a monotonous, relentless monologue – when as a country, and a world, we need to be having a conversation, as Noam Chomsky observed. Wonder why some Brits have been whipped up into a frenzy of racism recently? Because they are fed a toxic drip feed of lies by the media and their puppet politicians working towards an agenda of command and control.

Who owns the media? Three companies own 71% of national newspaper circulation in Britain. Of this, Rupert Murdoch owns *The Sun*, *The Times*, *Sunday Times*, the Press Association (plus *New York Post*, *The Wall Street Journal*, *The Australian*, Fox News and many more). Five companies own 81% of all UK local newspaper circulation.* The BBC is expected to act as a counter-weight to biased media, but Cardiff University researchers found that:

- Whichever party is in power, the Conservative party is granted more air time.
- On BBC News at Six, business representatives outnumbered trade union

* www.mediareform.org.uk/who-owns-the-uk-media

spokespersons by more than five to one, 11:2 in 2007 and by 19:1 in 2012.

- When it comes to the financial crisis, BBC coverage was almost completely dominated by stockbrokers, investment bankers, hedge fund managers and other City voices. Civil society voices or commentators who questioned the benefits of having such a large finance sector were almost completely absent from coverage.*

Carl Sagan, 1934-1996, once said, "The visions we are offering our children shape the future. It matters what those visions are." Never has it been more vital for us to collectively decouple ourselves from media brainwashing. I therefore urge you to:

1. Check who owns what you are viewing/reading.

2. Educate yourself but treat the information with a healthy pinch of salt.

3. Ask if its effects are toxic? Take a break and switch off. Your attention is an investment in their corporation.

4. Discriminate. Your trusted media may not be so 'independent'. See Professor Noam Chomsky on media propaganda.** Education and discrimination are powerful tools. (No surprise then that further education in Britain, excluding Scotland, is becoming ever more inaccessible for low income families.)

5. Support independent media by giving your custom to intelligent, independent news sources, magazines, websites and channels. They are often free or just the price of a cup of coffee.

6. Tell your friends about trusted sources. It is tough surviving out here.

* downloads.bbc.co.uk/bbctrust/assets/files/pdf/our_work/breadth_opinion/content_analysis.pdf
** www.youtube.com/watch?v=suFzznCHjko

The passing of Bill Mollison, the co-originator of the permaculture concept, is like a vast tree falling in a forest. The reverberations have been felt all over the world. He stood so tall over the canopy and now he is gone. Fisherman, beachcomber, farmer, scientific researcher, lecturer ... Bill was a polymath who gave up a promising academic career to teach permaculture and then train permaculture design teachers all over the world. He didn't want permaculture to be constrained by qualifications or formal education. He instead created an open source training for everyone and threw out thousands of seeds across the globe in the shape of permaculture practitioners and teachers. Today there are millions of us: 260 strategic organisations in 126 countries, and many thousands of projects in 140 countries.

I recently had the pleasure of teaching a course with Looby Macnamara, author of *People and Permaculture*, and one of the pioneers of the newly emerging 'social permaculture' movement that applies permaculture principles and processes to our human dimension: personal, in groups and in society. I am fascinated by patterns – in Nature, within our thinking and in human society – and Looby often refers to the concept of 'pattern disruption'. I have begun to observe its effects in many aspects of my life and in society at large. Pattern disruption can be destabilising, but it almost always forces the emergence of the new.

Take that great tree falling in a forest: it creates the influx of light under the canopy and an opportunity for seeds to germinate and saplings to grow, resulting in greater biodiversity and resilience. Although it may appear like a catastrophic event, it is Nature's way of ensuring natural succession. In societies that suppress pattern disruption, we experience stagnation and collapse. History shows us that these societies are unable to adapt to resource depletion or adopt new ideas that could ensure survival. They get stuck in negative ideologies and behaviours or are polarised by competing political beliefs that cannot deliver regenerative strategies.

Bill Mollison was an ultimate pattern disruptor. He began life in 1928 in Tasmania, a place that still feels very remote from Europe. Born into a rural community where few wore shoes, he spent his early life in what he described as a 'dream', deeply immersed in the natural world. His working life was spent in the bush or at sea, fishing and hunting for a living until, in the 1950s, large parts of the ecosystem in which he lived began to disappear. First, fish stocks became seriously depleted, the seaweed began to disappear and the old growth forests started being extensively logged. "The Japanese have come to take away most of our forest. They are using it for newsprint. I notice that you are putting it in your waste paper basket." Bill became a scientific researcher and then an academic, but I believe that his childhood and working life in Nature allowed him to experience a very different reality to the 'civilisation' that is intent on destroying our ecosystems. It enabled him to see the world in a completely different way from most people.

"I withdrew from society about 1970 because I had been long in opposition to the systems that I saw were killing us. I decided it was no good persisting with opposition that got you nowhere. I thought for two years. I wanted to return to society, but I wanted to come back only with something very positive. I did not want to oppose anything again and waste my time." Bill was determined to find a positive solution and it emerged as permaculture design, modelled on the ethics of earth care, people care and fair shares, and the application of the principles that sustain the cycles of healthy ecosystems.

Bill, uncompromising, irascible, the tough and tireless Indiana Jones of the alternative culture/agriculture world, was an excellent pattern disruptor. He didn't only challenge and disrupt the patterns of the status quo – of business, academia, politics, and the market economy – he also challenged the patterns of his co-originator, David Holmgren, and his subsequent students and followers. He was not a comfortable mentor and nor did he 'play the game' to get ahead and build 'influence' for the global movement he helped spawn. Nevertheless, he has left us an extraordinary legacy: in his aphorisms, books and in the many open source YouTubes he made.

"We are faced with an absolute choice: we can build the sort of cities we are building, continue to accumulate resources and power to run around like blowflies in cars, and be killed before long. Or we can live easily on the Earth. It's possible for us to construct biological systems that work,

it's well within our capacity … It's up to you, it's entirely up to you." May Bill's legacy continue to disrupt the destructive patterns of our global culture until we switch to regenerating our planetary ecosystems. As he often observed, "The solutions are embarrassingly simple."

2017 is the year we celebrate 25 years of publishing *PM*. It is an event that Tim and I neither anticipated nor dreamed of, but here we are. My first job in this editorial is therefore to express our gratitude by acknowledging the many people and organisations who have supported us over a quarter of a century. To all the people who have contributed articles, solutions, letters, reviews, photographs, artwork, without your vision, originality and practical experience, we would not be where we are today. To all our subscribers (both individuals and institutions), your support and encouragement are invaluable. To our advertisers, thank you – you help us to reach further out into the world. To our distributors, both print and digital, thank you for your faith in us and for the long arms of your logistics. To all the shops, cafés, libraries and other outlets who stock us, thank you and may you thrive in a difficult environment. To the people who have worked for *PM* past and present, it's been exciting as well as challenging, thank you for your service to the movement. To *Permaculture* magazine North America, thank you for taking the baton and giving birth to a new *PM* baby! To the Permaculture Association (Britain), thank you for asking us to start *PM* in 1992 and for your support over the years. To all the permaculture teachers and course convenors, thank you for spreading the word. To The Sustainability Centre, thank you for giving us a home. Lastly, to all you wonderful people who use your heads, engage with your hearts, and then act,

thank you for building a global movement that is going from strength to strength.

I am just back from the Oxford Real Farming Conference (ORFC), two days of inspiration, information and practical sharing of regenerative agriculture, horticulture, food sovereignty and policy. Started as an alternative to the 'other' industrial ag conference run by the NFU, it is one of the best and most holistic events I have been to. I am buzzing with the calibre of the talks, the power of the network, and the generous and friendly atmosphere.

The last session I attended was 'Farming and Metaphysics', chaired by Colin Tudge (co-founder of the Campaign for Real Farming), with Tom Gorringe, a Christian and Emeritus Professor of Theology at Exeter University, Justine Huxley, a Sufi from St Ethelburga's Centre for Peace and Reconciliation, and Rabbi Jonathan Wittenberg from North London Masorti Synagogue. It was a departure for ORFC and inspired a wide ranging and erudite discussion about the role of religion, spirituality, land ownership and radical change in our relationship to the land.

I asked: I believe that a growth in consciousness is the mechanism to begin a paradigm shift to a more resilient, regenerative and kinder world. Could the panel give the audience their advice in how we might grow consciousness? To paraphrase the answers: We are living at a time that resembles 1933 in terms of the rise of the Far Right and the brutality of neoliberalism. Corporations without ethics, industrial agriculture, land grabbing, and the disenfranchisement of the peasantry are rife globally. These are powerful forces. It is essential that we, who represent regenerative, healing, sustainable, enlightened, ethical practices, support each other and speak out in the world. We must not be inert. We are called to be radical. We can create change by engaging our heads with our hearts and then acting from that place. It is of great importance to nurture our love and connection with the Earth, to treat it as sacred in our daily practice, and devise ways of sharing insights and practical actions as widely as possible, whether we are farmer, horticulturist, gardener, policy maker, teacher, parent … Jonathan Wittenberg spoke movingly of Hans Jonas' final lecture, delivered days before he died, in which he spoke of the next revelation as coming not from Sinai or Gethsemane, but from 'the outcry of mute things'. We are hearing that cry now and need to respond with all our mettle.

Your belief system is your personal choice. I am not prescribing or projecting anything on to you. What I am suggesting is that irrespective of belief, let's help each other to become the people we want to be. Let's develop our own practices that bring us closer to Nature, make us more capable of listening and reflecting, more supportive of each other, and more able to act with greater wisdom and good effect in the world.

Recently, I used social media to take a pulse of my friends' lives. I asked them: "What is on your minds right now? What is important? What is calling you?" I was fortunate to receive answers from all over the world that were thoughtful and generous (no cat videos!), and I was heartened by the replies.

Many people are delighting at the rhythms of the changing seasons, making hugelkulturs, biochar, compost, planting, bottling, designing new phases of their lives using permaculture ethics, developing grassroots communication and decision-making processes, studying and evolving tropical and temperate regenerative agriculture systems, looking at community business models, considering pathways to new paradigms of living, being kind to vulnerable relatives, cycling, simplifying, downshifting, appraising, acting … It was inspiring to hear their stories and share their energy.

I also heard my friends' grief, both personal and in relation to the wider world. They wrote of the brutality of the political right, rising nationalism, plummeting levels of social care, the shift away from renewables and back to fossil fuels, planetary ecocide, the disintegration of the vast Larsen C ice shelf, rising sea levels, the threat to coastal cities worldwide … These are the issues that keep us awake at night. I am grateful to my friends who took the time to comment and the consideration taken with their replies. I felt their presence and read and reread every one. I found them comforting, even when they expressed despair and pain, because they expressed my despair and pain, and that of many others. We shared an empathy.

They asked why I wanted to know? When I look at the human world I mourn the ecocide we are committing on this planet. I feel sad about the extreme craziness of our world, the reversal of all the climate stabilisation policies in the USA, Britain's narrow, arrogant path, the inevitable violence and war that occurs as resources dwindle and power struggles erupt in the places where imperialist superpowers have interfered … I seriously wonder whether there will ever be a widespread adoption of all the sane, gentle and intelligent ways of living on this Earth that permaculture gives us. Will thuggish ignorance expressed by an unconscionable lust for money, sectarianism, and nationalism dominate all our landscapes? Will the grip of the controlling one percent continue to tighten, impoverishing the 99%?

Yet when I hear my friends' stories, I hear about the joy of connection with Nature, their hope and practical activism, and their focus on becoming more conscious, better human beings. This personal story is so completely opposite to the world at large. I am held in a dichotomy, stretched between a deep love of Life and respect for all the people who so positively try to live their dreams, and the appalling negativity of the few mad men and women who seem to be running this planet.

We wouldn't be human if we didn't have times of doubt that we cannot make a difference. I asked my friends what they are thinking and how they are focusing their energies because I needed to hear their voices and feel held and supported by a sense of community. I asked because I need to respond appropriately to what is happening in the world and find my own sense of balance. In taking their pulse, I was reaching out to my virtual yet powerful global community.

Preoccupied with how we should respond to world events, I asked two visionaries what keeps them going. One is Rob Hopkins, co-founder of the Transition Movement. The other is Tim Mead, pioneer of an independent organic brand of dairy products (in a world where the organic market is being bought out by Big Brother globally). These kind and clever men are very different but their answers both give voice to their energy, the capacity to renew themselves, their sense of place and their appreciation of family and community. As we teeter towards chaos and energy descent, I will be asking other visionaries how they maintain momentum. I think we all need to hear these stories to reset the balance.

There are many voices in this movement. They represent another powerful community of like minds who are trying to find balance, reframe ideas, learn new skills, take practical action, and empathise with each other. They show us that we are not alone by generously sharing their insights, experiments, projects and information. They offer us pathways to a better world and they give me hope and a sense of relentless determination. They enable this magazine to be a special kind of healing balm. Please enjoy.

# 93 | Autumn 2017

I am fascinated by natural springs. They are a result of surface water seeping into the Earth and filling a recharge area like a cave or aquifer (a geologic layer of porous and permeable material such as sand and gravel, limestone, or sandstone, through which water flows and is stored). When an aquifer is confined by impermeable rock layers in certain orientations, hydrostatic pressure can force water upwards through a network of cracks and fissures and the water eventually emerges at the surface. These are called artesian wells. Non-artesian springs flow from a higher elevation through the earth to a lower elevation and exit in the form of a spring, using the ground like a drainage pipe. Other springs result from pressure from an underground source in the earth, in the form of volcanic activity. The result can be a hot spring.

I live on the South Downs in southern England near the rising of the River Meon. Here the chalk ridge of the Downs forms a great natural amphitheatre beneath the South Downs Way. The rainwater seeps down through the permeable chalk into the aquifer. At the bottom of the bowl, where the groundwater table intercepts the surface, water emerges upwards out of the ground. The Meon rises in a muddy patch of yellow flag irises and then quickly, within a short distance, becomes a wide stream that flows out, is fed by more springs, and swells into a river on a steeper gradient. It feels miraculous, such is the vigour of its rising.

It is no wonder that our ancestors regarded natural springs as 'holy wells', sacred places revered for millennia. They were named, associated with legends and were attributed with healing qualities. They were reputed to cure illness or make the barren fertile. More prosaically, before mechanised sewage treatment systems and piped water, the most foolish thing a community could do was to dry up their life giving spring by poor land management or poison its water. Water is life and we all live downstream.

Our lives can be likened to rivers. Our birth is as miraculous as the rising of a spring in the landscape. Once we have arrived, with the right conditions, our growth gathers pace and we flow outwards into our lives. We merge with other streams and the river of our lives becomes a confluence. Ideally, in full flow, we are in full relationship with our family, friends, colleagues and our community. The latter isn't just the human world. If we are to become fully functional, actualised human beings, we need to be in relationship with the natural world as well. Here we can learn the lessons of life as effectively as we learn them in our relationships with fellow human beings. Here also can be our sanctuary from life's inevitable challenges and difficulties we encounter.

As our lives flow, significant rites of passage occur, like streams and rivers in confluence. These need to be consciously honoured in ways that mark them appropriately so that we carry forward the lessons they provide. Modern society is often poor at honouring and indeed understanding rites of passage. Part of our journey towards a more permanent culture is to develop our skills at celebrating these rites. We need to bring their significance into our consciousness. The final rite is the great transition, when our individual lives have taken their course and merge back into the source, like rivers to the ocean.

Tim and I are at the point of a number of confluences. Twenty-five years ago, *Permaculture* magazine was born, coming into our lives with a great surge of power, like an emerging spring, changing the way we thought and lived. At that time, I had two books in print, but my writer's life was put on hold when I started to edit magazines and the first books in the world about applying permaculture to temperate climates. Now I am breaking my silence with this new book, *Fertile Edges*, published to celebrate those 25 years.

At the same time, my family's life events are converging. My eldest daughter has just married and we welcome a son-in-law into our family, a creative, talented musician. My youngest daughter has completed her education, graduating with the highest honours. Her final year was spent exploring regenerative agriculture, permaculture, carbon sequestration and climate change solutions with words and photography. It is beautiful to watch the next generation step forward into their power. May they flourish. The river swells and reaches out to the future as we continue to mark and celebrate the importance of all our relationships with gratitude for being a part of this flow.

# Endpiece

I am not a person naturally given to retrospectives. I prefer to look forward, not backwards, and to be as fully in the present moment as I can. That way, I don't get to miss anything interesting! So the process of writing and editing this book has been contrary to my nature. Having said that, it has helped me to assess, and even retrieve, parts of myself that I may have inadvertently discarded in the rush of life or because they have pained me. I hope that for you too, this revisiting of historical events, the sense of time unfolding in these pages and seeing the ideas from the fertile edges growing in power and acceptance, have encouraged and given you hope. At the beginning of the book, permaculture was an intimate affair; now it is a global movement. Tomorrow it will be central to the principles and practice of regenerative development, a key tool for reversing, not just slowing down climate change, and part of enlightened policy for many governments. Already it is accepted as common sense by the current Secretary-General of the Commonwealth, Baroness Patricia Scotland. The Commonwealth's 52 member states account for a third of the world's population and Patricia Scotland intends to make their voices count in all UN climate negotiations.

At the beginning of this book, I wrote about Einstein's theory that humanity is capable of quantum shifts in consciousness if just 10% subscribe to new ideas. What seems set in stone and irrevocable today is yesterday's Berlin Wall lying in pieces, no longer dominating the landscape and dividing people. At the moment our collective story is tired, wrought with anguish, division and destruction. We need a new story more than ever before and the story that will shape the world is so close. As Arundhati Roy said, "Another world is not only possible, she is on her way. On a quiet day, I can hear her breathing."

People ask me how I have maintained my vision and energy during all these years. It is a mixture of stubbornness, not wanting to admit defeat and of having a sanctuary to return to when things get tough. I am, in essence, a lucky woman and not a day goes by when I am not grateful for what I have been given in this life. It is not to be taken for granted. Gratitude is one of the deepest secrets to happiness.

There are so many aspects of life that can feed us: great art, poetry, fine writing, a beautifully designed tool, a benign, energy saving/enhancing device, kindness, compassionate listening, courage … and the many other fine human qualities that exist, making the 10% of shared consciousness required for collective evolution not so far away. Perhaps we have to suffer a little more extreme posturing from our world leaders with the awful power of their weapons before the last 1% will be reached and we will change the paradigm we are in forever. For me, this shift is ever nearer, and what is happening in the world is both symptomatic and the catalyst. I too can hear that other world breathing itself into existence. My purpose over the years is to affirm this and encourage others to hold that vision.

# Acknowledgements

An editor can never thank adequately the people who buy, subscribe and advertise in their magazine, and the authors and creatives who generously support it with their articles and artwork. Without them, the discipline of a quarterly publication would quickly cease and these editorials would never have been written. I didn't write them alone. Behind the front-line of every issue is a group of people who advise, copy edit, proof, typeset, design, market and distribute each magazine. Patrick Whitefield, my mentor, was an invaluable ally until his untimely death in 2015 and the *PM* team have encouraged and honestly critiqued what I have written in every issue.

Within the permaculture movement I have had many teachers, some well known and others less so, but no less inspiring. I have also been lucky to be taught and befriended by people regarded as visionaries in the world like Joanna Macy, Rob Hopkins, John D. and Starhawk. I am indebted to them for the wonderful energy they bring into the world. May they continue to thrive and inspire change globally.

I have had other teachers outside the permaculture movement and some who are less visible, but no less valued. They have taught me to appreciate the deep lessons of Nature and of healing that are an ever developing subtext to my editorials. My gratitude to my two daughters, Hayley and Gail, who have grown from little girls to strong and beautiful women during the time covered in this book. Thank you for bearing with me when I was preoccupied with work or away from home, especially when you were growing up. I wish it could have been different, but you have never been absent in my heart. I am also blessed to have some wonderful friends and family who have stood by me, especially when times have been hard. Lastly, I must acknowledge the vision, stalwart support and editorial guidance of my husband, Tim Harland. Without his support, I would not be a writer or an editor.

# Books Published

During the 25 years of publishing *Permaculture* magazine, Permanent Publications has also published numerous books to help spread permaculture's message of earth care, peoplecare and fair shares, and to provide the practical knowledge and inspiration for people to live their lives in a caring and earth-centred way. The following is a list of the books that Permanent Publications has published during this time.

1990   *Healthy Business – The Natural Practitioner's Guide to Success,* Madeleine Harland & Glen Finn

1991   *The Barefoot Homoeopath – Health Care for the Whole Person,* Madeleine Harland & Glen Finn

1993   *Permaculture in a Nutshell*, Patrick Whitefield

      *The Permaculture Plot*, ed. Simon Pratt

      *Urban Permaculture – A Practical Handbook for Sustainable Living*, David Watkins

1994   *Permaculture Plants*, Jeff Nugent

      *Getting Started in Permaculture – Over 50 DIY Projects for House & Garden Using Recycled Materials*, Ross & Jenny Mars

1995   *A Wood of Our Own*, Julian Evans

1996   *The Basics of Permaculture Design*, Ross Mars

      *How to Make a Forest Garden*, Patrick Whitefield

1997   *Plants for a Future – Edible and Useful Plants for a Healthier World*, Ken Fern

1999   *Creating Harmony – Conflict Resolution in Community*, Hildur Jackson

      *Self Reliance – A Recipe for the New Millennium*, John Yeoman

2000   *Tipi Living*, Patrick Whitefield

2001   *The Woodland Way – A Permaculture Approach to Sustainable Woodland Management*, Ben Law

2002   *Sanctuary – A Guide to Finding a Different Relationship with the Land*, Elisabeth Edwards, Fionnuala O'Hare, Kath Simmons, Sue Weaver & Tamaris Taylor

2004   *The Permaculture Way* – Practical Steps to Create a Self-Sustaining World, Graham Bell

      *The Permaculture Garden*, Graham Bell

      *Eat More Raw – A Guide to Health and Sustainability*, Steve Charter

      *Designing and Maintaining Your Edible Landscape Naturally*, Robert Kourik

      *Building a Low Impact Roundhouse*, Tony Wrench

*The Earth Care Manual – A Permaculture Handbook For Britain and Other Temperate Climates*, Patrick Whitefield

2005 *The Woodland House*, Ben Law

*Ecological Aquaculture – A Sustainable Solution*, Laurence Hutchinson

2006 *Vegan Rustic Cooking – Through the Seasons*, Diana White

2007 *Beyond You & Me – Inspirations and Wisdom for Building Community*, eds. Kosha Anja Joubert & Robin Alfred

*Roots Demystified – Change Your Gardening Habits to Help Roots Thrive*, Robert Kourik

*Do It Yourself 12 Volt Solar Power*, Michel Daniek

2008 *The Woodland Year*, Ben Law

2009 *The Alternative Kitchen Garden – An A-Z*, Emma Cooper

*Birthrites – Rituals and Celebrations for the Child-bearing Years*, Jackie Singer

*The Living Landscape – How To Read and Understand It*, Patrick Whitefield

*Through the Eye of a Needle*, John-Paul Flintoff

2010 *Earth User's Guide to Permaculture*, Rosemary Morrow

*Gaian Economics – Living Well Within Planetary Limits*, eds. Jonathan Dawson, Ross Jackson & Helena Norberg Hodge

*Meat – A Benign Extravagance*, Simon Fairlie

*Roundwood Timber Framing – Building Naturally Using Local Resources*, Ben Law

*Sepp Holzer's Permaculture – A Practical Guide for Farms, Orchards and Gardens*, Sepp Holzer

*Find Your Power – A Toolkit for Resilience and Positive Change*, Chris Johnstone

2011 *Designing Ecological Habitats – Creating a Sense of Place*, eds. Christopher Mare & Max Lindeggar

*Grounds for Hope – Ways to Live Legally on Cheap Land in the UK*, Chrissie Sugden

*Permaculture Principles and Pathways Beyond Sustainability*, David Holmgren

2012 *Desert or Paradise – Restoring Endangered Landscapes Using Water Management, including Lake and Pond Construction*, Sepp Holzer

*The Moneyless Manifesto – Live Well, Live Rich, Live Free*, Mark Boyle

*People and Permaculture – Caring and Designing for Ourselves, Each Other and the Planet*, Looby Macnamara

*Permaculture Design – A Step by Step Guide*, Aranya

*Permaculture in Pots – How to Grow Food in Small Urban Space*, Juliet Kemp

*The Song of the Earth – A Synthesis of the Scientific & Spiritual Worldviews*, eds. Maddy Harland & William Keepin

2013 *Compact Living – How to Design Small Interior Space*, Michael Guerra

*Edible Cities – Urban Permaculture for Gardens, Balconies, Rooftops and Beyond*, Judith Anger, Immo Fiebrig & Martin Schnyder

*Letting in the Wild Edges*, Glennie Kindred

*The Log Book – Getting the Best From Your Woodburning Stove*, Will Rolls

*Outdoor Classrooms – A Handbook for School Gardens*, Carolyn Nuttall & Janet Millington

2014 *7 Ways to Think Differently – Embrace Potential, Respond to Life, Discover Abundance*, Looby Macnamara

*Around the World in 80 Plants – An Edible Perennial Vegetable Adventure For Temperate Climates*, Stephen Barstow

*Earth User's Guide to Teaching Permaculture*, Rosemary Morrow

*Edible Perennial Gardening – Growing Successful Polycultures in Small Spaces*, Anni Kelsey

*Manifesto of the Poor – Solutions Come From Below*, Francisco Van der Hoff Boersma

*The Permaculture Kitchen*, Carl Legge

*Sacred Earth Celebrations*, Glennie Kindred

*Septic Tank Options & Alternatives – Your Friendly Guide to Conventional, Natural and Eco-friendly Methods and Technologies*, Féidhlim Harty

*The Unselfish Spirit – Human Evolution in a Time of Global Crisis*, Mick Collins

*The Vegan Book of Permaculture – Recipes for Healthy Eating and Earthright Living*, Graham Burnett

*How to Read the Landscape*, Patrick Whitefield

2015 *Drinking Molotov Cocktails With Gandhi*, Mark Boyle

*Ecozoa*, Helen Moore

*Energy Revolution – Your Guide to Repowering the Energy System*, Howard Johns

*Getting Started in Your Own Wood*, Julian Evans

*Permaculture and Climate Change Adaptation – Inspiring Ecological, Social, Economic and Cultural Responses for Resilience and Transformation*, Thomas Henfrey & Gil Penha-Lopes

*Trees for Gardens, Orchards and Permaculture*, Martin Crawford

2016 *How to Permaculture Your Life – Strategies, Skills and Techniques for the Transition to a Greener World*, Ross Mars

*The Permaculture Book of DIY*, John Adams et al

*Zen in the Art of Permaculture Design*, Stefan Geyer

2017 *Forest Gardening in Practice – An Illustrated Practical Guide for Homes, Communities and Enterprises*, Tomas Remiarz

*No Dig Organic Home and Garden – Grow, Cook, Use & Store Your Harvest*, Charles Dowding & Stephanie Hafferty

*Resilience, Community Action & Societal Transformation – People, Place, Practice, Power, Politics & Possibility in Transition*, Thomas Henfrey, Gesa Maschkowski & Gil Penha-Lopes

*Fertile Edges – Regenerating Land, Culture and Hope*, Maddy Harland

*The Minimalist Gardener*, Patrick Whitefield

*The Permaculture Guide to Reed Beds – Designing, Building and Planting Your Treatment Wetland System*, Féidhlim Harty

# Index

350 Movement 92
activism
    importance of 19-20
    non-violent 60-1
    sense of powerlessness 48-9
    violence in 52-3
    'wider vision' of 35-6
Agenda 21 33
agriculture
    and climate change 38-9
    post-war planning 13
    regenerative 141-2
agroforestry 13-14
Agroforestry Research Trust 90
Alfred, Robin 67
Allen, Paul 102
Aranya 97
Australian Permaculture Convergence 67
'Awakening Albion' walk 110-11
Balter, Gaylah 37
Bane, Peter 3, 116
Bates, Albert 106
BBC 19, 68, 88, 90, 131, 137, 145-6
Bell, Graham 118
Bell, Nancy 118
Bellamy, David 46
*Beyond You and Me – Inspirations and
    Wisdom for Building Community*
    (Joubert and Alfred) 67
Bhutan 68-9, 132
biochar 29
Black Permaculture Network 140
Blair, Tony 50, 60
Boardman, Brenda 74
Boyle, Mark 97
'Brown Tech' 89, 129
BSE outbreak 5
Bush, George Jnr. 33

Byrnes, Josh 67
Byron, George Gordon 95
Carnegie, Andrew 143
Carruba, Capra 85
Center for Public Integrity 99
Chikukwa Project 135
China 74-5
Chomsky, Noam 145, 146
Christian Aid 8
CJD 5
Clayfield, Robin 125
Clear, Mary 117
climate change
    and agriculture 38-9
    costs of combating 50-1
    and deep ecology 78-9
    and Gulf Stream 11-12, 42
    impact of 42-3, 50, 74-5, 112, 127
    and permaculture 21-2, 33-4, 72-3
    pessimism about 92
    predictions for 21, 23-4
    resistance to solutions 31-2, 99-100,
    137-8
    responses to 70-1, 88-9, 92-3, 106-7
*Climate Change Scenarios for the United
    Kingdom* (DEFRA) 23
Climatic Research Unit (UEA) 99
*Compact Living – How to Design Interior
    Space* (Guerra) 116
Co-operative Bank 62
*Convenient Truth, A* (film) 73
co-operation 143-4
Copenhagen Conference 92, 99
Cow, Peter 125
Crawford, Martin 90
Curitiba 74
*Dancing Wu Li Masters, The* (Zukav) 48
Daniek, Michel 67

Darwin, Charles 143
*Day After Tomorrow, The* (film) 42
deep ecology 78-9
Depleted Uranium (DU) 40-1
*Descent of Man, The* (Darwin) 143
*Designing Ecological Habitats: Creating a Sense of Place* (Mare and Lindegger) 97
Detroit 136
Devereux, Paul 111
*Disturbing the Peace* (Havel) 65
*Do It Yourself 12 Volt Solar Power* (Daniek) 67
Doherty, Darren 97
Dowding, Charles 125, 129
Duhm, Dieter 72
*Earth Care Manual, The* (Whitefield) 29, 123
Earth Summit (2002) 33
East Timor 30
Ecocide Act proposal 107, 108-9
ecovillages 30, 37, 44-5, 84-5
*Edible Forest Gardens* (Jacke and Toensmeier) 30
Edwards, Emily D. 89
Einstein, Albert 5
energy systems
    energy descent 54-5
    importance of mixed 46-7
    protests over 60-1
English Nature 38
*Essence of Permaculture* (Holmgren) 29
*Eyes of the Wild, The* (O'Hanlon) 119
*Farm for the Future, A* (TV programme) 68, 88, 90, 131-2
Fern, Ken 3
Findhorn 30, 44
Flowerdew, Bob 7
Francis, Robyn 67, 125
Friends of the Earth 62

*Future Scenarios* (Holmgren) 129
*Future Starts Here, The – The Route to a Low-Carbon Economy* (Friends of the Earth *et al.*) 62
Gaia Education 30, 68
*Garbage Warrior* (film) 88
*Gardener's World* magazine 7
*Gardening With Soul* (Balter) 37
genetically modified (GM) food 38-9
Global Ecovillage Network 30, 84, 106
Goldsmith, Zach 19
Gore, Al 71, 72
Gorringe, Tom 149
*Grand Designs* (TV programme) 29
Great Turning movement 85
*Green Gold* (film) 135
Green, Tim 67, 88, 131-2
Greening Campaign 76-7
Guerra, Michael 116-17
guerrilla gardening 117
Gulf Stream 11-12, 42
Hafferty, Stephanie 125
Haiti earthquake 102
Hanh, Thich Nhat 49
Harland, Gail 97-8, 125, 154
Harland, Hayley 97, 125-6, 154
Harland, Maddy
    1996-2002 3-4
    2002-2006 30, 31, 56-7
    2007-2009 68-9, 90-1
    2010-2013 97-8, 110-11
    2013-2017 125, 154
Harland, Tim
    2002-2006 31
    2007-2009 68-9
    2010-2013 97-8, 110-11
*Harvesting Water, the Permaculture Way* (film) 67

Harvey, Bert 127
Havel, Vaclev 65
Higgins, Polly 107, 108-9
holidays 80-1
Holmgren, David 3
  and Bill Mollison 148
  on 'Brown Tech' 89, 129
  and ethics of permaculture 145
  and origins of permaculture 6, 26, 133
  publishes *Essence of Permaculture* 29
Holzer, Sepp 104-5, 120
Hopkins, Rob 3, 152
  April Fool on permaculture website 132
  on post-carbon future 84
  starts teaching permaculture course 29
  and Transition Movement 29
Hosking, Rebecca 68, 88, 90, 131-2, 137, 141-2
*How to Make a Forest Garden* (Whitefield) 3
Huxley, Justine 149
*Inconvenient Truth, An* (film) 71, 72
Incredible Edible Todmorden 117
indigenous peoples 133, 134
Intergovernmental Panel on Climate Change (IPCC) 38, 50, 71, 92, 99
International Permaculture Conference (IPC) 125, 134, 137, 139
International Permaculture Convergence 29, 67, 125, 134, 137, 139
International Society For Ecology and Culture (ISEC) 84
Iona 118-19
Iraq 29, 40
Isle of Wight 80-1
Jacke, David 30
Johnstone, Chris 99
Joubert, Kosha Anja 67

Joyce, Graham 110
Jung, Carl 5
Keeping, Will 60
Kemp, Juliet 116
Kindred, Glennie 70, 119
King, Martin Luther 92
*Kinsale Energy Descent Action Plan* 29
Kinsale Further Education Centre 29
Kyoto Agreement 50
LaDuke, Winona 27
landscapes 110-11, 118-19, 141
Law, Ben 29, 59, 82, 97, 101, 115
Lawton, Geoff 29, 67
Leahy, Gillian 135
Leahy, Terence 135
Leggett, Jeremy 71
Lichtenfels, Sabine 72
Lindegger, Max 67, 97
Liu, John D. 135, 136, 137
*Living Landscape, The* (Whitefield) 67
'Living With The Land' (film series) 137
Lovelock, James 46
Maathai, Wangari 139
MacArthur, Ellen 80
MacLeod, David 129-30
Macnamara, Looby 97, 125, 147
Macy, Joanna 52, 70, 72, 78, 82-3, 85, 89, 110
Mandela, Nelson 136
Mansfield, Michael 109
Mare, E. Christopher 97
Mayo, Ed 35-6
McCarthy, Michael 50
McCloud, Kevin 29, 137
McCurdy, Robina 125
Mead, Tim 152
media bias 145-6
Meier, Professor 38

Minghella, Anthony 80
Mobbs, Michael 67
Mollison, Bill 3
    death of 147-8
    and ethics of permaculture 145
    influence on Harland family 31
    and origins of permaculture 6, 133
    on permaculture 25, 58
*Moneyless Man, The* (Boyle) 97
*Moneyless Manifesto, The: Live Well, Live Rich, Live Free* (Boyle) 97
Monsanto 38
Moore, Phil 137
Morrow, Rosemary 67
Murdoch, Rupert 145
National Trust 38
New Economic Foundation 60
*New Internationalist* 67
*No Dig Home and Garden* (Dowding and Hafferty) 125
Norberg-Hodge, Helena 84
nuclear energy 46, 60, 61
O'Connor, Phillip 111
O'Hanlon, Eleanor 119
older people 84-5
organic farming 13, 15-16
Oxfam 7
Oxford Real Farming Conference (ORFC) 149-50
Page, John 73
*Paradise With Side Effects* (film) 84
Parry, Bruce 137
Peace School Mirja 72
Peak Oil 48, 54-5, 62, 63, 67, 88-9
*People & Permaculture* (Macnamara) 97, 147
*Perennial Vegetables* (Toensmeier) 67
Perez, Roberto 67

permaculture
    1996-2002 3
    2002-2006 29-30
    2007-2009 67-8
    2010-2013 97
    2013-2017 125, 134
    and agricultural planning 13-14
    and climate change 21-2, 33-4, 72-3
    description of 133
    design principles 6, 25, 58
    educational aspect of 58-9
    ethics of 145
    and indigenous peoples 134
    observation in 21
    and organic farming 15-16
    origins of 6
    and politics 145
    practical applications of 35, 59, 86, 112-13, 135-6
    self-critiquing 139-40
    societal aspects of 5, 17-18, 120-1, 145
    and sustainability 7-8, 25-6
    and Transition Movement 3, 62-3
    in urban setting 116-17, 136
*Permaculture Activist* 3
*Permaculture Design – Step by Step* (Aranya) 97
*Permaculture: A Designer's Manual* (Mollison) 25, 36
*Permaculture Handbook, The* (Bane) 116
Permaculture International Research Network 139
*Permaculture* magazine 3, 9-10, 31, 126, 149, 154
*Permaculture in a Nutshell* (Whitefield) 3
Permaculture People 137
*Permaculture in Pots – How to Grow Food in Small Urban Spaces* (Kemp) 116

*Permaculture – Principles and Pathways Beyond Sustainability* (Holmgren) 3, 36
Permanent Publications 3, 9, 29, 63, 67-8, 97, 125
Permatil 30
*Plants For A Future* (Fern) 3
Pugh, Sarah 136
Reij, Chris 120
renewable energy 46-7, 54-5, 60-1
*Resource Book for Permaculture* (Permatil) 30
Reynolds, Michael 88
Richards, Mark 97
Rio Summit (1992) 33
rites of passage 153-4
Rokke, Doug 40-1
Roof, Nancy 56
*Roundwood Timber Framing* (Law) 97, 101
Roy, Arundhati 155
Royal Society 38
Royal Society for the Protection of Birds (RSPB) 38
Sagan, Carl 146
Scotland, Baroness 155
Seed, John 52
self-reliance 86-7
Seven Generations Principle 114
Shawa, Mary 67
Simm, Clive 17
Simpson, Lauren 137
Smit, Tim 137
social governance 37
South Downs Experience week 127-8
Stapley, Christina 17
Starhawk 60, 125
sustainability
    code for 129-30
    and permaculture 7-8, 25-6
    teaching children about 114-15, 127-8

Sustainability Centre, The 3, 9-10, 97, 101, 114-15, 127-8, 149
*Symbolic Landscape* (Devereux) 111
Tamera Peace Research Village 46, 72, 104-5
*Thinking Like a Mountain* (Seed) 52
Tinker's Bubble 6
Todmorden 117
Toensmeier, Eric 30, 67
Transformational Media 115
Transition Movement
    and Greening Campaign 76-7
    growth of 63
    on Isle of Wight 80
    and permaculture 3, 62-3
    and post-carbon future 84
    start of 29
*Travels In Dreams* (Mollison) 3
Tudge, Colin 137, 149
Tyndall Centre for Climate Change 62
urban permaculture 116-17, 136
Village Farm 141
Ward, Barbara 99
water 153
Weapons of Mass Destruction (WMD) 40-1
Wedig, Harald 29
Whitefield, Patrick 3, 29, 43, 67, 123
Wilson, John 135
Wittenberg, Jonathan 149, 150
*Woodland House, The* (Law) 29
*Woodland Year, The* (Law) 67, 82
World Bank 60
Wrench, Tony 17
Yeo Valley 131
Zard, John 17
ZEGG 44
Zimbabwe 135
Zukav, Gary 48

# Subscribe to
# permaculture International
## practical solutions beyond sustainability

*Permaculture* magazine International offers
tried and tested ways of creating flexible, low cost
approaches to sustainable living

**Print subscribers have FREE digital and app access
to over 25 years of back issues**

To subscribe, check our daily updates
and to sign up to our eNewsletter see:

# www.permaculture.co.uk

See our North American specific edition at:
## https://permaculturemag.org

# Books to empower your head, heart and hands

   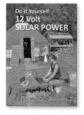 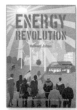

    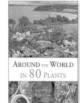

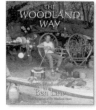   

For our full range of titles, to purchase books
and to sign up to our eNewsletter see:

## www.permanentpublications.co.uk

Also available in North America from:
**www.chelseagreen.com/permanentpublications**